Don Messer's Violin:
Canada's Fiddle

Li Robbins

Don Messer   Photo: Canadian Broadcasting Corporation

Geo. **Heinl** & Co. Limited   201 Church St., Toronto, Ontario M5B 1Y7   (416) 363-0093

Just as there is a cloud of mystery that surrounds the sound and appearance of some violins, so in other situations it surrounds the maker; such is the case with **Don Messer's Violin**.

The printed name of "Pierre Boisvin" on the label inside the violin is a spurious attribution at best. I cannot find a maker of that surname listed in any of our archives. However, there was a French maker of note active in Paris during the 1700's by the name of "Pierre Boivin". In the late 1800's it was common practice for French ateliers to seize license, if you will, by taking names of past makers, altering the spelling slightly so as not to create a legal situation and to slip these labels into instruments bound for the Americas. Many first class makers worked for large French shops and created violins of quality for clients abroad. A finished instrument was made ready for export with the insertion of a label. Such was the case with Don Messer's violin. Given its placement, the label – clearly – was inserted after manufacture.

So who made Don Messer's Violin? After much study and examination, with the aid of black light and endoscopic equipment, the violin has revealed a clue in the form of a signature or "Maker's Mark". The "MAKER'S MARK" in the form of two arcs in black ink can be seen in the bottom of the peg box when viewed from above. "𝓜 ".

Perhaps, this was a last minute decision by the maker before surrendering the instrument so as not to leave his creation orphaned. It is clearly visible when a light is shone into the peg box at a point between the fingerboard nut and the "G" peg. The authorship I do not know, as I have not previously recorded such a device. Nor do the archives of my ancestors shed any light on such a design. In closing, it is my opinion that we will likely never know the artist who created **Don Messer's Violin**.

R. W. Heinl

Aug 5d /05

Letter of expert opinion on Don Messer's violin supplied by Geo. Heinl and Co. Ltd.

Library and Archives Canada Cataloguing in Publication

Messer, Don, 1909-1973
Don Messer's Violin: Canada's Fiddle / Li Robbins

ISBN 0-660-19489-9

1. Messer, Don   2. Musicians (Music) – Canada – Biography
3. Leahy, Frank   4. Canadian Broadcasting Corporation

I. Robbins, Li   II. Title.
III. Title: Don Messer's Violin: Canada's Fiddle

Published by the Canadian Broadcasting Corporation

Design and Layout by: Scott Kletke Designs
Consulting and Printing, Arnold Huffman – TCG Total Concept Group.

ISBN 0-660-19489-9

Canadian Broadcasting Corporation
P.O. Box 500, Postal Station A
Toronto, Ontario M5W 1E6
Phone: 416-205-7376
Fax: 416-205-2376

http://www.schools.cbc.ca

Table of Contents

Author's Note

It was a great pleasure, honour and responsibility to have the opportunity to tell some small part of the story of Don Messer and His Islanders. Many people were involved with this project, and I would like to take this opportunity to thank some of them.

For sharing their stories, opinions and memories, a huge thanks to the following people:

Dawn (Messer) Attis	Waldo Munro
Ann-Marie Chamberlain	Gary Nielsen
Don Chamberlain	Manny Pittson
Barry Chamberlain	Don Reed
Ned Landry	Johnnie Reid
Bill Langstroth	Ken Reynolds
Cleaver MacLean	Don Tremaine
Ruby MacLean	Emma Treadwell
Ruth Munro	April Verch

Their insights, along with archival material, formed the backbone of this narrative.

I owe much appreciation to my editor, Shirley Rennie, my agent, Jackie Joiner and to Barbara Brown of the CBC's Merchandising Department and indexer Carol Fordyce.

For their patient assistance in enabling the research for this book to be done in record time, thanks to: Barry Smith, Darlene Brine, Ginny Clark and the rest of the staff at the Nova Scotia Archives and Records Management; Liliane Hunkelel, Laurie Nemetz and Maureen Kennedy of CBC's Visual Resources Department; Michele Melady and the staff of CBC's Reference & Design Library; Rob van der Bliek, Librarian, Sound and Moving Image Library, York University, and Ric Heinl of Geo. Heinl and Co. Ltd.

As well, a special note of thanks to Frank Leahy. His passion for Don Messer's violin, and for the music of Don Messer and His Islanders, was the moving force behind this book.

Preface

We're going to visit Waldo Munro — Frank Leahy and I. We're both a little nervous; Waldo is one of the few members of the Islanders still alive, a terrific piano player we both admire. It hasn't been easy to arrange the visit, though. His health is troubled, and there have been other troubles too, the kind that arise out of the business of music, the stuff of rumour and misunderstanding. So the interview has been tentative, but now it's finally set.

It's a perfect spring day in Halifax, the sort of day where it's easy to forget that just a few days ago high winds whipped rains through the city so severely it made local news headlines. It's impossible to forget the history of the place though; the cab driver makes sure of that. He points to the cemetery where *Titanic* victims are buried, and as we dip past the harbour he details the events leading up to the Halifax explosion of 1917. What he doesn't know, and what we're too preoccupied to tell him, is that we're on our way to speak to someone who's also a part of the history, not only of Halifax, but of the Maritimes and all of Canada.

Frank is bringing the violin of course. *The* violin, the one that Don Messer liked best to play, through all those years of dances and radio shows and television broadcasts and tours that criss-crossed Canada; the violin that wasn't played for a quarter of a century after Mr. Messer passed away, until it came into Frank's hands. Now it sits silent in its case between us on the car seat, looking somehow too small to be so significant.

When Frank hands the violin to Waldo it looks too small to him too, he's dubious; he shakes his head. It isn't until Frank shows him the "tiger striped" pattern of the wood on the violin's back that Waldo believes it's really Messer's violin. Or maybe he only truly believes it when Frank takes out the bow and plays a bit of *Rippling Water Jig*, the tune's cascade of notes a signature of Messer's repertoire, and of the legacy of the Islanders.

The interview begins. Waldo sits deep in a huge chair, his face altered by the years and by Parkinson's, but something in his eyes seem as alive as it did in those 1960s *Jubilee* programs when he'd pull off flawless runs on the ivories. Soon he gets up from the chair, walks slowly to the dining room table, where the violin sits in the open case. He looks at it, a long, hard look. It's easy to imagine the years falling away, the many memories it must hold for him. Perhaps the old violin is a symbol of all the ups and downs that went along with playing in a band that was one of the best loved music groups ever to exist in Canada.

Frank's hoping that Waldo will agree to play a few tunes. He does play still, although it pains him that illness makes it impossible to execute the fleet-fingered right-hand work of old, or the fabulous stride in the bass with the accuracy that made his playing so impeccable. But despite his hesitation you can tell he'd like to try a tune or two with Frank, and with Don Messer's violin.

In the music room the walls are filled with framed pictures of the band — including one of those classy shots with the band members' signatures beneath their photos. There's Don, Marg and Charlie, and Duke, Rae, Cec and Warren, they're all there. And Waldo himself, of course. Now he sits at the keyboard beneath the photo, facing a music stand that holds some of the old covers of his solo recordings — on one he's billed as Waldo "Thumbs" Munro. (Not all thumbs though, that's for sure.)

Frank starts in on *Rippling Water Jig*, taking it at quite a clip. After a bar or two Waldo is right with him. Next it's *Rubber Dolly*, then *Blue Mountain Rag*, *Londonderry Hornpipe* and before you know it they've worked their way through half a dozen tunes. Waldo's time is as pure and settled as ever — as old barrelhouse and boogie woogie musicians would say, "He has a left hand like God." Frank looks nervous and blissful all at once, but Waldo seems as calm as the warm spring Halifax day itself.

Later, in the taxi heading back downtown, Frank will tell me how Waldo's playing made it easy for him, secure. He'll also admit that at first he got so nervous he was "blowing it big time." But in fact, as they play it doesn't matter that Waldo can't execute every technical feat, or that Frank makes the odd fluff. What matters is the music, which sings out with the same honest appeal as it did when Don Messer and His Islanders played it back in 1939 on CFCY in Charlottetown. What matters on this day, as they wrap up with Don Messer's signature closing tune, *Smile The While*, is that the music is being played, that the music is still alive.

— Li Robbins, Halifax, May 2005

Foreword by Frank Leahy

I grew up in a small country town called Teeswater, nestled in the drumlins of southwestern Ontario, Canada. During my formative years there were two things I spent my time doing.... playing hockey and playing music, fiddle music, that is. I had a hockey stick in one hand and the violin in the other, although not usually at the same time.

Music in my world came in the form of country/folk genres with a little bit of jazz thrown in for good measure. There was no formal training available where we lived so, under the direction of my Dad, I was told to copy or emulate the best fiddle player by listening to his LPs, to his radio shows and by watching him on one of the two TV channels that came into the house.

The name of this best fiddle player was Don Messer.

I can still hear my Dad saying, "If you want to be the best, match Don Messer."

So needless to say, I was listening to and replicating all of Mr. Messer's licks as I grew up, and still to this day from time to time my own playing is refreshed by listening to the magic of Don Messer and His Islanders.

When I was selected by the Messer estate in 1997 to engage in the resurrection of Don Messer's Violin, I had no idea there was so much substance behind the man and his music. It has been an astonishing discovery for me over the last five or six years, analyzing archives, and talking to living members of the Islanders, as well as to some of their close friends, and to the band members' children. Every one of these groups has their own story of Messer and his Islanders, which made the journey even richer.

I have a tremendous amount of respect for Don Messer, not only for his musicianship but also for his vision, perseverance and passion. Don Messer and his Islanders took 300-year-old fiddle tunes and made them popular and, in doing so, created happy hearts throughout Canada and the rest of the world. They presented this uniquely Canadian style of music in a way that was not seen before and has not appeared since. They made it their own. They made it Canadian. They were the pioneers of "music variety" for CBC radio and CBC TV. Their unrelenting consistent touring across Canada and the northern United States is still a testament of their dedication to their uniquely Canadian art form.

The book you are about to read centres around Don Messer's Violin. After all, it is the fiddle that is at the centre of all this. Li Robbins carefully describes the origins and career of Mr. Messer and his violin from the humble beginnings in Tweedside, New Brunswick, to the glory days when he starred in the number one rated TV show in Canadian broadcasting history. You are wonderful, Li.

As the custodian of Don Messer's Violin, my goal is to carry on the Canadian tradition established by Don Messer. Mr. Messer has shown me the way ... using Canada's Fiddle, I will continue from where he left off.

The torch has been passed. Watch for me.

— Frank Leahy

Chapter One

"OH, HOW HE COULD PLAY!"

Birth of a Violin

This violin was built to endure, its wood well-aged for strength, and assessed for acoustic properties. Folklore has it that the quest for perfect violin wood was sometimes conducted under less-than-scientifically controlled conditions — by men wandering through the woods tapping trees with mallets, or isolating the logs that rang out most vibrantly as they careened through watery chutes in their voyage down mountain slopes. While less dramatic methods may have been used to select the wood for this violin — maple for the back, and spruce for the front — the raw materials must have met with satisfaction, since the wood arrived at Mirecourt, famed French centre of violin making, located south and east of Paris, not far from the German border.

In Mirecourt, circa 1890, a skilled (but devious) luthier began to create the violin from that wood. He wanted to claim the instrument as his own, but even more than that he wanted money, the most money he could get from its sale. So (perhaps with a twinge at orphaning his own creation) he fixed a false label on the inside, visible to prospective buyers through the *ff* holes on top. This label claimed the instrument was made by Pierre Boisvin, at his atelier on rue de Grenelle, in Paris. Although there appears to be no luthier of that name on record, there was one with a very similar name, in France in the 1700s — Pierre Boivin. Clearly the fake label was intended to trick an unwary buyer into believing the instrument was made by the latter Pierre, at his prestigious Paris address, thus increasing the value of the instrument. Still, in the end the luthier couldn't resist surreptitiously adding his real mark to the violin — two little arcs in black ink at the bottom of the violin's peg box, marks no one would notice

1

— at least, not until more than a century later, when they were revealed through the use of black light and endoscopic equipment.

It's unlikely the violin's maker would ever have predicted a future for the instrument that would include such scrutiny, let alone guess at the music it would one day play. If anything, perhaps he imagined the violin playing melodies from popular operas, or a Saint-Saëns violin sonata, logical choices for a Paris-born violin of the day. However, this violin, as it turned out, wasn't going to spend its life in the hands of a classical violinist in France; this violin was bound for Canada.

The precise reason the violin left Europe is as much a mystery as the name of the man who made it. Given his attempts to obscure the violin's true origins, it seems probable he intended it to be shipped to North America to be sold new, far away from any potential suspicions as to its provenance. Probable, but not a certainty. It's also possible that the violin belonged to some lonely soul who decided to join relatives from a previous wave of migration, or to an adventurer, lured by the Canadian government's advertisements abroad, enticing settlers to the "last best west."

Whatever the reason, the violin left France and made a transatlantic crossing, a much easier feat at the turn of the 20th century than it had been a hundred years before; improved health measures and the transition from sail to steam power made the voyage much faster and safer. Still, crossings were always potentially risky, and in some cases, infamously fatal. The *Titanic* took less than three hours to sink in 1912, leaving about 1,500 dead, 121 of whom were buried in the Fairview Cemetery in Halifax, Nova Scotia.

But the violin suffered no such dire fate on its voyage to Canada. Its journey may have been utterly tranquil, rocking gently in its case, protected from the salty ocean spray. However, if the violin was in the possession of someone who liked to play — and to a captive audience — it may have been taken from its case, may have felt the weight of the bow as its master struck up a lively dance tune. It's easy to imagine that this jaunty sound would have inspired at least a few passengers to spring to their feet and dance — since, after all, what would be a more fitting response to the instrument that would one day become Don Messer's violin.

The Runt

They called him "the runt." That's what he got for being the youngest, and perpetually small for his age. And with five older sisters and five older brothers, a nickname like that was probably inevitable. Maybe it hurt his feelings at first but you'd never know — in later years he'd smile when the moniker came up. His position in the family pecking order and his stature (as a grown man he was 5 foot 6 inches, according to his 1931 driver's licence) may even have made him more determined to excel, since "the runt" started playing the violin when he was only four years old.

Donald Charles Frederick Messer came into this world on May 9, 1909, in Tweedside, New Brunswick, a small farming community southwest of Fredericton, the child of John and Margaret Messer. The Messer family farm was typical of York County, with a mix of cows and chickens and cultivated land. The children helped out, from haymaking and milking to gathering eggs and feeding the hens that laid them. But this quiet life on the Messer family farm was severely disrupted by the death of Margaret Messer in 1921. After his mother died, twelve-year-old Donald's older sisters mothered him — Janie, who was 26 years older than he was and already out of the family home, and his sister Emma, his favourite family accompanist, who was still living on the farm.

Before Margaret Messer's death, life for the Messer family was peaceful, by all accounts. The farm's location, within walking distance of Oromocto Lake, was paradise for a small boy. The Messer children liked to head to the lake whenever they could, sometimes taking a short cut through the woods, eager to fish for lake trout and leap into the bracing cold water on hot summer days.

On cold winter days there was school in a one-room schoolhouse, and on Sundays there was always church. Both sides of the family were staunch Presbyterians of Scottish descent, and had lived in Canada since early in the 19th century. Originally the Messer family was thought to have been German — the word Messer is German for "knife" — but the Messers of New Brunswick were Scottish-Canadian through and through.

Sunday was a day of rest in the Messer family, a belief instilled so deeply that it perhaps cost Don Messer dearly, half a century later, when he refused to have his famous television program moved to Sunday evenings. He felt that a show of fiddling and dancing on a Sunday would seem as wrong to his audience as it did to him, so the show was moved instead to Fridays, a less advantageous time. Perhaps, when Messer made this decision, he recalled an incident from childhood, when his father had caught him playing a jig with his sister Emma on the Sabbath, a transgression for which they were both sternly reprimanded.

When he was still a boy called Donald though, being told to "hush" on Sundays was quite a task. He was, after all, just a kid, a kid who would sometimes sneak off to the lake on a hot Sunday afternoon; there he could learn to swim, and dream of playing the violin.

The Harvey Quadrille

Questions of a national Canadian identity, and, more to the point, a national economic policy, were among the most pressing of issues for Canadian politicians post-Confederation. Prime Minister John A. Macdonald's national policy of 1879 was presented as the economic adhesive sealing the country together, east to west. Initial results in the Maritimes were mixed, but by the turn of the century the picture was largely one of economic loss, not gain, as a result not only of government policy, but also of the unstoppable forces of industrialization — notably the collapse of the wooden-ship-building industry.

As for family farms such as the Messers', they grew smaller as times grew tougher. There were health scares as well as economic woes — a mere few weeks before Donald Messer was born, the government of New Brunswick appointed a commission on the spread of tuberculosis in the province. People needed a break from all of these woes, and one of the best ways to push aside your troubles was to listen to music, and to dance.

Don Messer's Violin: Canada's Fiddle

The heart and soul of community music-making was the violin, as Don Messer sometimes preferred to call the instrument. But he also used the more familiar term favoured by fans of country and folk styles of playing — the fiddle. And when Messer was a boy, certainly most folks would have said it was the fiddle that rang out at family get-togethers, parties, barn-raisings and frolics, as dances were often called. Not to say there weren't other kinds of music being played; Saint John city can boast that in 1907, two years before Donald Messer was born, local musicians made history by being among the first in North America to accompany a silent moving picture. That was at a theatre owned by Walter Golding, buddy to Louis B. Mayer. There was classical music too, with ensembles such as the Saint John Choral Society. However, in the countryside, Scottish and Irish fiddle tunes ruled.

After school Donald Messer would rush home to play music with his siblings, his violin waiting for him on top of the family pump organ in the parlour. Music was the best thing going, next to fishing. It was also as much a part of daily life as doing his chores — his sisters and brothers sang in choirs, his mother sang Scottish tunes around the house, and his Uncle Jim Messer fiddled, as did Jim's sons. Two of his sisters could play piano and organ, and two brothers played violin. In fact, it was one of those brothers who unwittingly provided the final tantalizing enticement for the would-be fiddler Donald. One winter this brother went into the woods to work in a lumber camp, and not only did he leave his violin at home, he locked the case. It was an irresistible challenge for a determined young boy to unscrew the hinges, take the instrument out, and begin to play.

It's unlikely Donald Messer was only four years old when he got to the point of infiltrating his brother's violin case though, more likely he was a little older, with more manual dexterity and even more determination to play, perhaps already imagining his public debut. That happened when he'd reached the ripe old age of seven. Messer described the event to journalist Pierre Berton half-a-century later, in an interview in 1966:

"I played my first barn dance when I was seven ... I remember playing for the first dance. They set me up on the kitchen table, I was so small, you know. Oh, it was quite an experience."

Soon the sight of wee Donald Messer (frequently perched on top of a box set on a chair) fiddling up a storm was not an uncommon sight. The boy loved it — the music, and the atmosphere. For him frolics were about family, and about having fun, and in later years Messer liked to recall those times: "They used to dance all night until morning. And the women folks would bring on pancakes. They'd cook pancakes, and fry pork and have a regular feast."

The tune that Messer remembered playing at his auspicious premiere was the "Harvey Quadrille", played over and over again, as the dancers seemed never to tire of it. But it was only one of many tunes he already knew, since even at seven he had "quite a repertoire." Quite a repertoire, Messer recalled, meant "perhaps a couple of dozen numbers."

Naturally, if he was going to play for the grownups, he felt he should have his own violin, and likely his brother wasn't a fan of having "the runt" borrowing his, either. So the older Messer boys bought their youngest brother his own instrument, picking it up from the T. Eaton company for $1.98; the princely sum also included a case. Still, like many violinists much his senior, Messer wanted more than one instrument on hand. When a seed package company held a contest promising a violin, Donald Messer went to work, as he recalled years later to Pierre Berton: "You'd sell so many seeds and for a prize you'd get your choice of a violin, or a camera or something like that. So I chose the violin. But when it arrived in the house and I opened up the package the violin was all in little pieces, all broken up. So I had to get another one."

Not even the arrival of a shattered violin could put him off, though. Soon he managed to buy one from a local tinker, costing somewhere between five and twelve dollars, as he would variously recall. Whatever the precise amount, it was money well spent, since it's likely that this was the instrument that became the teenaged Messer's ticket to commerce, as well as to good times. Soon he was playing wedding receptions and parties in the local settlements near Tweedside — places like Brockway, York Mills and Harvey Station. It was impossible to know exactly how much money he'd pocket at the end of a night though, since the amount depended on how happy the dancers were, and how much cash they were willing to part with. Any money was a help at home, but more to the point, he just loved to play.

Some years later, in a newspaper column Messer clipped for one of the scrapbooks he would keep all his life, an unnamed woman from Harvey Station remembered trying to chat with him at some of those dances.

"He was terribly shy then, you could hardly get a word out of him, but oh, how he could play!"

Beantown

If you lived in Boston in 1925, it would be difficult not to be aware of the ongoing dispute over the veracity of a famous local medium known as "Margery", a dispute conducted by two celebrities — author Sir Arthur Conan Doyle and conjuror Houdini. Their battle over whether or not "Margery" was in contact with the spirit world was as entertaining as the sale of Babe Ruth to the New York Yankees had been shocking, five years earlier.

This was the city Donald Messer first encountered when he moved to Boston at the age of 16. It was a city lacking the restraint of, say, Fredericton or Saint John, a city whose people made national news, but who were slow, Messer felt, to take to strangers. Still, it was his biggest adventure to date, and perhaps even at that age he sensed that adventures are not for the easily discouraged.

Messer was anything but. After having finished school two years earlier, graduating from grade eight, he continued to play for frolics and parties, but he also made a trip out west on a harvest expedition with one of his brothers. Still, he hadn't found any work to really grab on to, nothing that seemed substantial enough to make a life. So, following the path of many Maritimers with family in Boston, he headed to Beantown.

Two of his father's sisters lived in Boston, and he moved in with one of these aunts in Roxbury, one of the city's oldest neighbourhoods. Life in Boston wasn't always easy, but for Messer it was eye-opening — first because of a chance encounter with classical music, and second because of his growing attraction to another kind of medium that was indisputably real — radio.

W-Bees Knees

In the 1920s a radio station called WBZ in Boston broadcast baseball scores, farm reports, lectures and music — mostly classical and opera, but also music from popular stars such as Eddie Cantor. Around the same time that Sir Arthur Conan Doyle and Houdini were going at it over the question of spiritualism, the station also linked up with CKAC in Montreal to broadcast hockey games, no doubt a favourite with Canadian ex-pats. By the mid-1920s WBZ was so popular its nickname was W-bees-knees, slang for "the greatest!"

WBZ in particular and radio in general was a comfort to Messer. The city of Boston itself was overwhelming. When he arrived, a teenaged boy whose only contacts were a couple of aunts and a cousin, it might as well have been London, England for all the resemblance it bore to Tweedside. Speaking to writer Lester B. Sellick in the late 1960s, Messer recalled his emotional reaction:

"I found Boston a rather strange, cold place at that time; it was hard to make friends in the big city, close friends that is … I was lonesome for the family gatherings back home."

Knowing how to harness a team of horses or play *Haste to the Wedding* proved not to be marketable skills in Boston, so soon he found himself working at a succession of lowly restaurant jobs, finally landing a better-paid job as a receiving clerk at F.W. Woolworth Co. He worked hard at Woolworth's and began to slowly acquire more responsibility. But

Messer wasn't having the kind of fun he was used to at home, playing music for the kind of people he'd known all his life. Listening to the radio became the chief way he'd pass his spare time. He even picked up some new fiddle tunes from the radio, Irish numbers from a broadcast by a group called The Irish Minstrels. Messer became such a fan of radio that he visited the studios of WBZ and also a station called WEEI, where he met "a young chap from Prince Edward Island named Art McDonald," as he recalled later to Sellick. That young chap was to provide Messer's ticket to fame some 15 years on, by inviting him to become the musical director and orchestra leader at a feisty little radio station in Charlottetown, P.E.I., called CFCY.

Scales at Dawn

Sometimes opportunity arises where you least expect it. For Messer, it was in his aunt's own home. She had a roomer who turned out to be a professor of music, a Professor Davis. Davis, in a charmed coincidence, was also a violinist. Messer, in his interview with Pierre Berton, remembered the fateful day Professor Davis overhead him playing:

"...oh, he tore out his hair you know and said 'well this boy should be taking lessons. He's got a wonderful gift to play the violin. He's just got to take and learn the proper way.' So he introduced me to one of his pupils that taught violin, a Mrs. Hurter."

If this story were fiction, Donald Messer would have become a devoted student of classical music, eagerly anticipating the 12 or so lessons he took with Mrs. Hurter over the next year. The story would end with Messer as concertmaster of an orchestra. But fortunately for the history of Canadian music and broadcasting, Messer discovered he didn't like the formal studies.

"It was too monotonous playing the same things over again and over again," he said later. Still, he recognized that the lessons gave him new skills and technique, and that they were a conduit to meeting other young musicians. He became part of a small ensemble that sometimes played concerts in local churches, Messer in the first violin chair. Mrs. Hurter was teaching him to read music, but he still found it easier to have his fellow musicians "run through the number once," following which he would know the piece well enough to play from memory.

Although he disliked the pedagogy of western classical music after a lifetime of playing by ear, this dislike was outweighed by a desire that was to drive him all of his life. It was a craving to learn more about music, and about his chosen instrument, the violin. And there was something else too, something that people who knew him called his "perfectionism", or his "obsessiveness." Regardless of what psychological term you want to apply, the determination of Donald Messer was among the qualities that most profoundly shaped his career and ultimate fame. In those early days, it was enough to make him get up at dawn, before work, and practise his scales.

From Fish to Jewellery

There are various stories told in newspaper and magazine articles about Messer's return to Canada. He was homesick. He visited Saint John, and realized life in a Canadian city might suit him better than living stateside. He had been in the U.S. long enough that he had to make a decision about applying for American citizenship. It's likely all or any of these factors had an impact on his decision to go home. But there was another factor too, which he characterized in the interview with Pierre Berton as "a nervous breakdown." He described the circumstances leading up to this state of mind as calmly as he had talked about selling seed packages to buy a violin.

"At the time I was merchandising, for a chain store, in Boston. And I was very enthused over the work. I liked it very much. And I would work from early morning until late at night, and it just got too much … It's something you just can't explain, but it's something that comes over you, you know you've got to do something about it, you've got to get away and have a rest, and this is what I did."

He was still very young, after all, not yet 20, and getting up at five in the morning to practise, going to work all day, and frequently working nights as well, dressing windows in the store. He had few friends, and no close family at hand. No wonder it "just got too much." Ultimately though, in choosing to return to Canada he was, whether he realized it or not, choosing music.

He came home at the worst of times. The stock market crashed, and the Depression sank its teeth deeply into the economy of the Maritimes, in part because of the ensuing collapse of the market for fish. Many Maritimers who had previously headed west returned; the combination of the Depression and a long series of agricultural setbacks (including drought, grasshopper invasions and crop attacks by sawflies, cutworms and wireworms) was demoralizing. The result was a glut of labour in the Maritimes, and little available work.

People needed escape more than ever, given these fresh miseries, and again they found it through music, and through radio. By 1930 it was estimated that 500,000 Canadians were paying the annual one-dollar radio licence fee, and at that rate it was probably the cheapest entertainment going.

As for Messer, like most young men he took whatever work he could get, including a stint on the railroad. He also began what was to be a lifetime habit of trying to create his own luck. Clarinetist Rae Simmons, a long-time colleague of Messer's, said in a 1979 CBC radio interview that he'd heard Messer talk about all the kinds of ways he tried to earn money during the "dirty thirties."

"He even tried to sell fish. Which was crazy, isn't it? He bought fish and took it from house to house. The houses he took it to wouldn't have the money to buy it anyway. A dozen fish would only be probably in those days, maybe six cents for a dozen …"

Simmons also remembered Messer talking about going door to door selling coal. But Messer kept playing music too, with a small group that sometimes included piano player Hilda Humphreys and a singing fiddler named Jack Stevens, along with another musician named Carl Mason. None of these performers were with him for the long haul, but they provided a chance for Messer to try his hand as band leader, a role he was to claim for the rest of his life.

There were still dances to be played, of course, and he and his friends would whisk through tunes such as *Soldier's Joy, Top of the Cork Road, Wind Shakes the Barley, Beaux of Oak Hill* and more — spirited tunes guaranteed to lift heavy hearts. The money was poor, less than he had made as a young teen before the Depression. But performing on the radio, if you managed it cleverly, could provide another small source of income.

It began with Don Messer's brother-in-law, who persuaded a fish store in Saint John to sponsor a live radio broadcast on CFBO, the first radio station in the city. Ironically for Messer, a young man who loved radio, his debut was less than pleasant. He and a piano player (or perhaps a small group, on this point the story has some variations) went into the station and handed over a list of tunes they could play. The announcer hustled them into a room with a single microphone, read out the song list, and without further ceremony, abandoned them. So they began to play, assuming he would return in between songs — but the announcer didn't. For about fifteen minutes they just kept going, without anyone saying a word. Messer found the whole experience utterly unnerving, and doubted there'd be a repeat performance. But listeners liked what they heard, so much so that a Saint John jeweller wanted to sponsor more broadcasts. Messer didn't say no.

Radio was a ticket to a modest degree of fame, with potential for much more. In 1934, Donald, now shortened to Don, with a group billed as Don Messer's Old Time Orchestra, performed live-to-air at a prestigious radio exhibition held at a ballroom in Saint John's Admiral Beatty Hotel. ("You will be able to see and hear them actually performing before the 'mike' " stated a newspaper preview.) The music was a bonus for attendees, who could also browse through the exhibition, which featured "the last word in modern radio receiving equipment."

Messer had soon realized that, if he paid for radio time himself, and if he had more sponsors than needed to meet the station's rates, well, that's how he could turn a profit. A small profit, but a profit nonetheless. But from his WBZ listening days he knew what made professional radio and what didn't. What did was an announcer, someone to draw the public in. Fortuitously he encountered a man named Maunsell O'Neil at around this time. O'Neil was quite a cut-up, perfect announcer fodder, and he and Messer quickly teamed up, with O'Neil conducting his announcing duties in the guise of "Joe LeBlanc", an impersonation of an Acadian woodsman. This was a savvy choice at the time, given that woodsmen seemed to embody a curious combination of romance and comic sensibility — at least to those who never went into the woods. Early evidence of this dates back to 1921, when the Maritime Motion Picture Company made their first feature film, a drama about woodsmen, called *Big Timber*. (It starred an American, but locals were invited to appear as "burly lumberjacks." If, that is, they brought their own axes.)

One real-life woodsman was to become critical to Don Messer's success.

The Singing Lumberjack

"Lumberjack Makes a Hit," read the 1934 headline. "Radio listeners throughout the miles of scattered country served by the eastern network of the Canadian Radio Commission last evening heard the voice of Charlie Chamberlain … youthful musical discovery…"

The youthful musical discovery in question had been singing with Don Messer for about a month when this article was printed. After Messer recovered from his inauspicious beginnings on the air, he continued to perform on CFBO, which soon went by the call letters CHSJ. CHSJ was an affiliate of the two-year-old Canadian Radio Broadcasting Company, (CRBC), predecessor to today's Canadian Broadcasting Company (CBC), created by Prime Minister R.B. Bennett. The station generated a modest amount of programming carried across CRBC's network, including the programs *Fundy Fantasy* and *New Brunswick Breakdown*, the latter featuring Don Messer.

13

Years later, in 1960, CBC Television Information Services would recall how J. Frank Willis, then regional director for the CRBC, auditioned Don Messer as a solo artist for the network. According to this release, it was Willis who suggested Messer would do best to re-audition with a group. Messer brought in some of his musical friends, and the deal was sealed. Willis was quoted as recalling, "I am very gratified with the way things have turned out for Messer. His universal public support bears out my decision 26 years ago."

At first Messer called his group Don Messer and His Old Time Band, which was sometimes dubbed by the press as Don Messer's Old Tymers Orchestra, referring not to the youthful performers, but to the nature of the music they played. But whatever ensemble name Messer or the press fancied, there was no question radio was the going thing, the way to making the name Messer synonymous with musical talent.

"Something a little out of the ordinary in the way of entertainment is promised local citizens," read an article in the *Campbellton Graphic*, circa 1934, "when Don Messer's Radio Orchestra visits Campbellton tomorrow." The performances were to be accompanied by a buffet luncheon, and the group was described as being "justly [famous] over the radio," comprised of "leading artists in their line." It featured, of course, "the singing lumberjack."

Charlie Chamberlain, a.k.a. the Singing Lumberjack, inspired Messer to create a more memorable name for the group, the New Brunswick Lumberjacks, frequently just called the Lumberjacks. Messer and Chamberlain were both from New Brunswick, but Chamberlain legitimized the other half of the name, since he actually had worked in the woods. (Unlike the other men who floated through the group — early photos of the Lumberjacks show as many as 16 musicians, and sometimes the band reportedly had closer to 20.) But despite any romanticism attached to the notion of being a lumberjack, there was nothing romantic about how Charlie Chamberlain ended up in the woods. Chamberlain was one of six children; his father worked with the police department in

Bathurst, New Brunswick, and his mother worked at the local courthouse. His family was musical, all his siblings sang, and one sister, Effie, played piano for silent movies. His mother played in a more genteel setting — at church on Sundays. None of this would seem a likely starting point for life as a lumberjack. But Charlie Chamberlain's father died when he was nine or ten, and the family fell on hard times. One of the few ways he could bring in money was to go into the woods to work, so this is what he did, at first cleaning pots and pans and later trimming the trees when they fell. The work was seasonal, in part because trees could most easily be dragged out of the woods in winter, over the smooth glide of snow. Chamberlain continued to work winters in lumber camps throughout his teenaged years, but then he met and fell in love with a young woman named Lydia, nicknamed Petite-Belle, or Ti-Belle, and they started a family. He began hoping for a permanent way out of the woods, and the way out was through music.

The story of how Charlie Chamberlain and Don Messer met has taken on mythic proportions, and its precise history remains unclear. However, all variants of the story begin with Charlie Chamberlain on a train, leaving the woods to see his wife and infant child in Saint John. As was frequently the case throughout his life, wherever Chamberlain went he was playing guitar and singing to pass the time, and maybe to pass the hat and earn a little extra money as well. Somebody (his daughter Ann-Marie would later recall it was Bill Holden; fiddler and one-time Messer band member Ned Landry heard it was Maunsell O'Neil, and some newspaper accounts claimed it was a business man named Landsdowne Belyea) heard and was impressed by Chamberlain's singing. This somebody introduced Chamberlain to Messer and, some reports say, to a band leader named Bruce Holder. Apparently both leaders auditioned and liked the burly young singer. Messer was to recall in later years that the first song Chamberlain sang was *Lonesome Valley Sally*, and that "he had a wonderful voice." Chamberlain, who brought with him a repertoire of songs and ballads learned in the lumber camps, seems to have worked for both leaders for brief while, but ultimately gravitated towards Messer, becoming the band's larger-than-life front man, funny, gregarious and an unforgettable character.

Backing both Messer and Chamberlain, and with a personality no smaller than Charlie Chamberlain's own, was the man who played the upright bass, Julius "Duke" Nielsen.

Josh

Why the lanky bass player was nicknamed Duke is as much of a mystery today as why Don Messer often called him Josh. (In turn, Nielsen called Messer "Oscar," nicknames that persisted throughout their long history together.) Why Messer wanted Nielsen in his band is less of a mystery — the man was multi- and curiously-talented, he could play the banjo and the bass, he was a fire-eater, he could do magic tricks and he could wrestle tame bears, should the occasion arise.

Like Messer and Chamberlain, music was part of Nielsen's birthright — his father was a similarly multi-talented Dane, a photographer who had been a cornet player in John Phillip Sousa's band. Less happily, Duke Nielsen also shared the legacy of loss — he too had lost a parent while still very young. In Nielsen's case it was his father who had passed away, when he was around ten years old. His mother was unable to support the children, so Julius Nielsen and his sisters had to go into an orphanage. He wasn't there for long though, perhaps a year. And once he got out, he did what many boys of his age just dreamed of doing — he literally ran away with the circus.

Nielsen's circus training was a bonus for Messer, since novelty numbers helped draw audiences to shows. Messer was always interested in delivering what he believed his audiences wanted — he had a knack for figuring out how to please the people. In the 1930s pleasing the people meant variety, where music came first but a touch of vaudeville didn't come last. And what could ensure more variety than the occasional exhibition by Julius — the "human volcano" — Nielsen in between numbers?

"You'll stamp your feet when they play both new and old-time music," declared one poster for performances in 1937 and 1938. "You'll roar with laughter at the gags and antics." Nielsen supplied many of those antics in the early years, and in later years as well, adopting a persona called "Uncle Luke", donning an oversized fake mustache, a droopy hat, and exhibiting a penchant for a certain type of humour.

"What's worse than a wife with a wooden leg?" Uncle Luke might ask the eager audience. "I once had a wife with a cedar chest," he would conclude, to great guffaws.

But Uncle Luke emerged later. First there was just Julius "Duke" Nielsen, the lanky guy with the bass fiddle, the awkward instrument that had to be strapped to the running board of the Model A as the band traveled the Maritimes, seeking their fortune. Or at least, in those Depression years, seeking a way to keep body and soul together.

The Backwoods Trio

The New Brunswick Lumberjacks, with their cast of thousands, were an unwieldy group to take on the road, not to mention that the chances of anyone making a thin dime were considerably diminished as a result. But Messer with Chamberlain and Nielsen also worked as The Backwoods Trio, sometimes adding members to form a quartet, or a quintet, The Backwoods Five — all names being variants of Messer's latest radio show, *The Backwoods Breakdown*. (As the Backwoods Five they promised audiences "Musicians + Singers + Funsters," guaranteed to be "All New! — All Peppy!")

There were always plenty of musicians eager to jump in with Messer, whether he was playing in barns or renting halls for a couple of dollars a night. Regulars, in the early years, included two performers who were to become famous on their own — pianist Eldon Rathburn, who would one day be one of Canada's noted film score composers, and a young harmonica player named Ned Landry, later three-time winner of the prestigious annual Canadian Open Old Time Fiddler's Contest. But the trio were the canvas Messer's musical vision was painted on, and both Chamberlain and Nielsen were with Messer for most of his life.

Boston continued to play a part in the young musicians' lives throughout the 1930s. In fact one incarnation of the band had an early big break in the town that was "famed for its beans and codfish," as one 1935 article remarked. This squib was written in honour of the triumphant return of "Don Messer and His Lumberjacks" from the New England's Sportsmen's Show, held at the Mechanics Building in Boston.

The recommendation that Messer and his Lumberjacks represent New Brunswick at the prestigious event had come from on high, as Hector Charlesworth, chairman of the CRBC, approved of what he heard. The Sportsmen's show was both an excellent opportunity for the band, and for the government of New Brunswick. The New Brunswick representatives were emissaries or, to put it in the words of one journalist, they were to "extol the sporting and scenic attractions of their native province," thereby encouraging American fishermen into the wilds of eastern Canada. The band, attired in checked shirts and other suitably lumberjack-like garb, extolled through music — at this show and in subsequent performances at similar shows in Hartford, Connecticut, and at Madison Square Garden in New York City. And for members of the American public who weren't sure exactly where the musical woodsmen hailed from, at the 1936 show in Boston there was a large map of the province of New Brunswick, in which Saint John's relative position to various Unites States cities was clearly shown.

There were numerous fringe benefits arising from the Sportsmen's gigs. On some occasions they led to other engagements in New England, including one performance at the toity Brookline Country Club, where Messer and company performed in front of the Roosevelts. Another ongoing benefit was granted upon their return home in 1935, when CHSJ's fifteen-minute *Breakdown* program was increased to half an hour. Following their 1936 appearance, the Boston media started taking notice as well. In Howard Fitzpatrick's "Among the Studios" column in the *Boston*

Post on February 14, 1936, Fitzpatrick raved: "A new singing personality has invaded local radio circles in the person of Charlie Chamberlain, who made his debut over WHDH with the New Brunswick Lumberjacks during the Sportsmen's Show." That year the Lumberjacks also had a tryout with NBC radio. It would appear that the audition was not successful, although they did end up playing a short contract for WHDH, an unaffiliated Boston station, and — according to a "historical sketch" CBC radio issued in the early 1940s — about five other radio stations, including WBZ.

The capper occurred the following year though, at the 1937 Sportsmen's Show in Boston, when a scout for CBS radio's wildly popular *Major Bowes' Original Amateur Hour* heard them, and subsequently invited the group onto the program. Famous radio host Major Bowes, the *Toronto Star* reported in 1936, received 1,500 letters a day, from star-struck hopefuls desperate to get on his show. Most had day jobs: as dog catchers, fruit pedlars, elevator operators, beachcombers... anything, as long as they could make ends meet. "Holland-born hillbillies have played stone jugs, garbage men have sung grand opera..." reported the *Star*.

The *Major Bowes* appearance resulted in a particularly spectacular spinoff for Charlie Chamberlain, whose successful performance was rewarded with a spotlight at a club called the Silver Slipper. Jimmy Durante was booked there at the time, and was so impressed with Chamberlain that he gave him a Hollywood connection that resulted in a contract offer. But Chamberlain didn't want to leave the band, or his home in Canada.

Perhaps, as Pierre Berton suggested years later to Messer, the Lumberjacks were really ringers on Bowes' show, since they were already well on their way to a serious career in music. But Messer said no, they thought of themselves as amateurs at the time. Whether he was quietly pulling Berton's leg is hard to say. Regardless, after the band's appearance on Bowes' show Messer did not jump at an offer to take part in Bowes' travelling circuit. Not for 34 dollars a week — the money was too low. It wasn't just about money though, there were other considerations. After all, by this time Messer was a married man, with an infant daughter.

"Mrs. Don Messer, Farm Girl at Heart"

Years after the success of Messer's first performance at the Sportsmen's Show in Boston, his wife Naomi was typically described as "a friendly, unaffected brunette," or a "farm girl at heart," when newspapers, striving to figure out the woman behind the man wanted to know what made Mrs. Messer tick. But when Don Messer started courting his wife-to-be in the early 1930s, she was Naomi Gray, city girl, living in Saint John and training to be a nurse. They dated for a couple of years, sometimes spending months apart when Messer would return home to Tweedside to visit family and help with haying, or when Naomi (whom he nicknamed 'Nomas') would visit her family in Belldune, New Brunswick.

Don Messer, writing to Naomi in August of 1932 (mentioning he had gone to a dance but hadn't stayed long, since "my sweetheart wasn't there so of course I couldn't enjoy it") worried about the impending launch of his first radio show. "I am not sure when our program is going to start," he wrote, "Anyway I seem to dread it you know as I make so many mistakes." Signing off "oodles of hugs and kisses," Messer presumably went on the air sometime during the next year, and most likely without making "so many mistakes." Messer, a perfectionist from the start, would have practised too much to allow that to happen.

Perhaps he was feeling more confident by the following summer, since in August of 1933 he wrote to his Nomas (he also nicknamed her 'Nomie') saying "… this bachelor business is no good so I guess I will have to get hitched. How about it?" and signing off with a sweet little drawing of a stick man and woman hugging.

She must have said yes, because Naomi Dorothy Gray and Donald Frederick Messer married the following year. Money was, of course, an issue for the young couple — in the same letter containing his proposal, he mentioned making $1.75 from playing a dance, and wrote about his hopes that an upcoming private party would be "a help." But they started out with almost nothing. In fact, as their eldest daughter Dawn (Messer) Attis remembered being told, they were given a table and chairs and a bed from her Aunt Janie, and that was it. Naomi — who eventually was just nicknamed "Nom" — according to her eldest daughter, came from a family who, not atypically for the times, disapproved of musicians, and wedding gifts were not forthcoming.

Don and Naomi Messer's first child was born the following February, the little girl whose name, Dawn, would later inspire headlines such as "The Other Dawn Messer." But in her first year of life she was sometimes just called Dee Dee, by her mother at any rate, in letters Naomi Messer would write to her husband when he was on the road. It was a hard time for a young couple to start out, and to be separated made it harder still. In February 1936 Naomi Messer wrote to her husband in Boston regularly, filling him in on both domestic trivia and personal longings, or apologizing for spats they'd had, and always thanking him for the money he sent home. (On one occasion she outlined how she'd spent the eight dollars he managed to send — four dollars on the grocery bill, two dollars on the insurance, with plans to pay down the milk bill.) The need for money was a constant theme, as was their mutual loneliness.

"Every day of life I have a crying spell," she wrote on one occasion. "I am so lonesome but I will endure it as long as you are making some money." She saw her husband's music partly as a means to a financial end, but clearly she was also proud of his success; she wrote that at night she'd struggle to tune in the Boston radio station he was performing on, although usually she'd report back that the reception was "noisy." It didn't matter how much static there was though, a broadcast from Boston picked up in Saint John was still a link between the couple, and tangible proof of the respect even Americans were giving to the musical talents of Messer and the group.

Naomi Messer wasn't the only one writing letters to Don Messer during the winter of 1936. In a lengthy letter from a friend writing from Kirkland Lake, Ontario, in March of that year, the significance of the Boston gigs was duly noted, perhaps with a tinge of envy. "So you had a try out with the N.B.C.", wrote Messer's friend, a banjo player named Ray. "Well Boston is a Hell of a place to hang around in with no work and it is so hard to get." Mind you, Kirkland Lake wasn't a piece of cake in the work department either, although Ray, experimenting with "a chap that has one of those new electric guitars" suggested it was possible to "pull down pretty good." The Kirkland Lake dances paid around "four and five dollars a dance," he wrote, campaigning to get Messer to move north and form a band. But the Don Messer who would turn down Major Bowes' 34 dollars a week, a year later, certainly wasn't going to up stakes for Kirkland Lake. He was too busy planting the seeds for a future a little closer to home.

"Also the Only Dictating Machine Cylinder Manufacturers in Canada"

Since at least 1935, Messer (writing on behalf of his Old Tyme Dance Band) had been trying to get the RCA Victor Company interested in recording the group. Although the Artists and Repertoire department of RCA in Montreal was willing to entertain an audition, they weren't enthusiastic. They "certainly could not recommend" that Messer bring his "orchestra" to Montreal "solely on this possibility." The primary reason given was: "… with the remuneration derived from records today, it certainly would not be worth while." On the other hand, if he wanted to spend his own money he was welcome to make "twelve ten-inch single-faced records reproducing one selection" for 55 dollars (the price dropping to 40 cents each, for orders over 500). RCA's attitude was disheartening, but Messer continued to scheme. After the success of the 1937 Sportsmen's Show and the CHJS radio show, it finally clicked. He had solid interest from the Compo Company Limited ("Canada's Largest Record Manufacturers, Also the Only Dictating Machine Cylinder Manufacturers in Canada").

The first records Don Messer and his band made were recorded live from — where else — the radio. The Montreal-based Compo recorded the Saint John-based Messer and company off-air throughout the summer of 1937, releasing 78s on the Melotone and Starr labels in the autumn. Their recording technique proved to have a few wrinkles.

"Last Saturday night was hard luck night," wrote the manager at Compo on August 12, 1937. "The first number we recorded was too long, otherwise it would have been exceedingly good. The second one came on so fast on account of number three being so short, that we muffed it."

Technical traumas aside, Messer's recording career was under way. As for tunes being too long — that would soon cease to be a problem, as Messer honed his skill at timing music to something of a science.

Recordings were one more way to spread the word about the band's music, but RCA may have been right when they suggested it wasn't a big money maker. In a royalty statement from Compo in June of 1939, Messer received a quarterly royalty cheque for $3.48. Still, it did mean that at their one cent "per part" rate they had sold 348 recordings for that period.

Of course none of this — recordings or live performances — would have been possible without Messer's two crackerjack accomplices, Chamberlain and Nielsen, and without his singular musical talents, honed daily by playing his favourite French violin.

Chapter Two

"THE WAY DOWN EAST MUSIC OF DON MESSER AND HIS ISLANDERS"

As Light as a Feather

When Don Messer's sister, Emma Treadwell, at 101 years of age in 2005, held her brother's violin for the first time in who knows how many years, she was astonished at how light it was. "As light as a feather," she said.

It's true that a violin is a startling combination of fragility and power, typically weighing somewhere around 450 grams, but able to produce over 100 decibels of sound. (As a point of comparison, a rock concert can peak at over 130 dBs.) Of course it's not a question of whether or not Don Messer's violin can compete in intensity with The Rolling Stones; the individuality of the instrument is what ultimately matters. Any violin is the musical fingerprint of the artist who plays it, and although Don Messer owned around a dozen violins in later years, there was one he always preferred to play.

This was the violin that was safely beside him on the car seat, in 1935, when the trailer hauling the other instruments caught fire someplace outside Buctouche, New Brunswick — a less-than-stellar moment on a tour of the North Shore. This was the violin that recorded *Petronella, Half-Penny Reel* and *Lamplighter's Hornpipe* for Melotone Records in 1937, the violin that sang out across the Maritimes throughout that decade, at events such as the Lobster Carnival in Pictou, Nova Scotia, causing local press to note that "thousands acclaimed Don Messer's Orchestra." This violin was played by Don Messer for four decades on some of the most popular radio and television shows in Canadian history.

But even though Don Messer's violin was such an essential part of his life, how he came to own the instrument isn't entirely clear. At different times and in different interviews, Messer said he bought it either in 1926 or in 1930, for a sum of about one hundred dollars. If the 1926 date is true it's most likely it was purchased in Boston. But memory plays tricks with precise dates, and 1930 seems more probable, since in 1926, 17 year-old Messer was unlikely to have been in a financial position to spring for a hundred-dollar violin. Regardless, his daughter Dawn recalls that the story of "how-Dad-got-the-violin" was always told this way:

"Dad saw it in the window of a music store in Saint John, and he admired it, and wished he had it. Mum was working at the time, and she went in unbeknownst to him and purchased the violin on time. That was what Mum and Dad always said ..."

It may be that in interviews Don Messer didn't want to publicly recall the forces of the Depression that had him so short-handed that his wife bought him the violin "on time" for five dollars a week, as his daughter would remember being told. But however and whenever the instrument was acquired, the French violin had clearly met its match. As had Don Messer.

You Couldn't Buy a Job

In the Depression, as the saying went, "you couldn't buy a job." Don Messer took a different approach. He called it, on various occasions, "creating your own work," which in his case translated to playing radio shows, and dances and parties — any place a fiddler was required. In the 1930s many of the live dates Messer played around the Maritimes were on what was nicknamed the Kerosene Circuit, since these hamlets hadn't yet "got the electric in." Travelling the twisting roads of the Maritimes was a challenge, with The Backwoods Trio or Five squeezed into the Model T with their instruments, frequently stopping to tie a lantern to its hood when the headlights died, as they were prone to do on the darkest of nights. Things improved when they graduated to a Model A, with its wide running board, perfect for carrying Duke Nielsen's bass fiddle. But that presented another liability, as proven on one occasion when a close brush with an oncoming vehicle sheared the instrument right off. (Nielsen literally picked up the pieces and began a lifelong sideline of repairing the bass.)

The dangers weren't only on the road, however, sometimes they were at the dances themselves, usually late at night after the crowd was liquored up, and someone picked a fight. On one memorable occasion the band was packing up to leave when a group of fellows came along and threatened them — unless they kept playing. Another time there were so many people pounding the floor that the hall began to sag, and the centre posts holding up the ceiling fell right out. (Fortunately, the ceiling held on its own, and everyone just kept dancing.) Ned Landry, who played "mouth organ" and eventually fiddle with Messer, would recall that in those early days anything could and did happen. Once, riding in the home-made trailer the band used to carry its instruments (Landry being smaller than the others), he got so cold that his feet were like blocks of ice. "Better take your boots off," Messer advised. Kind-hearted Charlie Chamberlain blew on Landry's feet until he could feel them again. Another time the trailer unhitched, and Landry and the instruments ended up in a jumble. That time, he recalled with a laugh, the men were more concerned about the fate of the instruments.

"Creating your own work," and travelling with the men and boys who were part of that work was not without its economic perils as well. In Black's Harbour, New Brunswick on one occasion, they didn't take enough at the door for anyone to scrape together a cup of coffee — so they were paid in cans of sardines. But Messer was looking for something better than being paid in fish. Ultimately he found it, via that ever-growing success story, his friend the radio.

"Girdle the Globe in a Flash"

Radio technology continued to improve in the late 1930s, in terms of reception, newsgathering abilities, and the radios themselves — new push-button models in cars prevented a driver from being distracted by all that dial-spinning. Yes, radio had come a long way since disbelief met Guglielmo Marconi's pronouncement in 1901 (the year the young Italian received the first transatlantic radio transmission at Signal Hill,

Newfoundland), that radio would "girdle the globe in a flash." Although reporting on news events (such as the first days of the Dionne Quintuplets, the mine collapse at Moose River, Nova Scotia, the coronation of King George VI) was one of the reasons that newspapers, sensing the competition, snapped up the ownership of many radio stations, music still reigned supreme. In Canada, music played on radio had an early and significant start when Canadian Reginald Fessenden played the first recording ever heard on radio in 1906, Handel's *Largo*, followed by his own performance of *O Holy Night* — on the violin.

As for the public broadcaster, in its early days music dominated its airwaves. But the CRBC was a highly political animal right from its beginnings in1932, setting its course as the national institution everyone liked to love or hate. What sort of music and how much should be played was soon a topic for some debate. In 1936 the CRBC became the CBC, meaning Hector Charlesworth — the CRBC chairman who had endorsed Messer's appearance at the Sportsmen's Shows, and in general approved of home-grown Canadian music — was out of a job.

Aside from issues about what would be on the public airwaves, there was another inescapable reality for the young national broadcaster — most of the million Canadians who had radios were listening to the private stations, or to American broadcasting. Consequently the CBC began a campaign to expand its network programming and to build new stations, including one in Halifax. The station's construction was delayed though, caught up in squabbles over whether CBC should be expanding programming, or facilities. This delay was to forever alter the course of Don Messer's life. In the first year of CBC's existence, 70 per cent of what was broadcast was music, popular and otherwise, but within a few years this dropped to about 50 per cent — right about the time that Don Messer was petitioning the soon-to-exist station in Halifax.

On March 6, 1939, Messer received a response to his campaign to launch a program on the new station, written by George Young, Regional Program Director at CBC Halifax. Young was clearly trying to keep all irons in all fires, saying he couldn't accept the *Backwoods Breakdown* program at the present time, "pending the opening of the new station," but he really hoped Messer was going to keep in touch. But Messer wasn't twiddling his thumbs waiting for his lucky day with CBC Halifax. Why would he, when there was a savvy private station showing interest, one that was also a CBC affiliate, CFCY in Charlottetown, Prince Edward Island.

The Friendly Voice

In 1907, two years before Don Messer was born, a teenager named Keith Rogers was spending most of his free time messing about with bits of wire and brass screws in his parents' Charlottetown home. Rogers had this notion that one day voices and music would travel effortlessly through the air, and that if he persisted, he might become a master of "the continuous waves," as they were sometimes called. In 1925, after years of mucking about with coils and condensers, his dream came true — he was granted the first commercial radio licence in P.E.I., for the station CFCY.

Visitors to the early CFCY studios (also known as Keith Rogers' house) noticed a decidedly non-technological oddity — a number of backless kitchen chairs. But music-lovers would guess right away at their purpose, since of course it was easier to bow a violin sitting on a chair without a back. And fiddling was popular on CFCY — in fact the fiddler Lem Jay was the station's very first live performer. (Until that time music had only been broadcast "mechanically", that is, via a record player in front of a microphone.) Lem Jay became a regular, and he was apparently such a toe-tapper that he wore a bare spot on the carpet beside the microphone.

By 1935 Rogers wanted to turn his attentions to liaising with private broadcasters across the country, so he hired a man to oversee the day-to-day operations of the station. That man was L.A. "Art" McDonald — the same McDonald Don Messer had met at WEEI in Boston in the late 1920s. McDonald made many contributions to CFCY, but the two he is best remembered for are creating the station's slogan, "The Friendly Voice of the Maritimes," and hiring Don Messer to be the station's "Musical Director and Orchestra Leader."

Operator's Reel

From the start Messer was an avid collector of fiddle tunes, violin miscellany, and fiddle recordings. But a fascination with music was never at the expense of his family. To move from his native New Brunswick with Naomi and their two small daughters (Lorna Messer was born in 1937), and all their worldly possessions, was a risk. Mind you, the Depression underscored that simply being alive was a risk, and then, as it drew to a close, there was an even bigger risk facing the world. Canada entered the Second World War on September 10, 1939.

At least upping stakes to accept CFCY's offer was a risk with a steady pay cheque attached to it, presuming the new show worked out, and Messer was determined that it should. So for $12.50 a week Messer accepted the offer. Charlie Chamberlain came too, and both men and their families arrived in Charlottetown in Model A's overflowing with possessions tied every which way to keep them from flying out of the vehicles. The third member of the Backwoods Trio wasn't with them at first, but Duke Nielsen would eventually move to the island as well, becoming part of Messer's new band, Don Messer and His Islanders.

Messer could at least reassure himself and his family that without question the people of P.E.I. loved old-time music, as fiddling had a strong tradition on the island. In 1926 the Strand Theatre in Charlottetown had held a fiddling competition (the winner guaranteed a performance in Boston) that was so successful special train excursions had to be laid on, to bring in the crowds. Also, Messer and Chamberlain had performed on the island in the past, on some of their jaunts around the Maritimes, and were already known to audiences.

The island had its own bands before Messer and company arrived; among the best known leaders was George Chappelle with his group The Merry Islanders, who performed regularly on CFCY. A piano player named Jackie Doyle had played with Chappelle, as had a clarinet and sax player called Rae Simmons, and a drummer named Bill LeBlanc. It seems that Chapelle and CFCY station boss Art McDonald didn't always see eye to eye. On top of that, when war broke out a number of Chapelle's band members joined up. All good timing for Don Messer, who scooped up Simmons, LeBlanc and Doyle for his band, and "borrowed" a key word from the Merry Islanders name to give his group a new identity.

Real Hoe-Down Specialists

On November 11, 1939, the radio audience heard Art McDonald sign on for the first time with what was to become a trademark intro:

"From the studios of CFCY in Charlottetown, Prince Edward Island, it's the way down east music of Don Messer and His Islanders!"

The first tune they played was one of Messer's own compositions, marked on the cue sheet as *Operators*, its full name *Operator's Reel*. (Messer, while not prolific, did compose a number of well-liked fiddle tunes.) A selection of jigs, reels, songs, waltzes (plus a march and a breakdown) saw the program to its concluding number, *Roll Out the Barrel*.

McDonald soon realized he'd chosen well in offering Messer the job. Not only did he get an excellent musician, he had also hired a man whose anxiety over making any mistakes ensured he was highly unlikely to make them — and a man who did his utmost to ensure his band members upheld this standard as well. The show caught on, and graduated from once a week to twice-to thrice-weekly broadcasts. As for the band, as with all of Messer's early groups, members came and went until it eventually settled into the core membership that would become so well-loved in later, television years. But in the early years on the island performers came and went, including bass player Cecil Santry, pianist O.K. Presby and singer Tex Cochrane, among others. Messer was seeking constancy, it just took him a while to find the men who were ready and willing to supply it.

CFCY had built its reputation in no small part on traditional east coast music. It had also built its ever-evolving facilities on the strengths of its staff, their vision, and sometimes their brawn. Not long after Messer and His Islanders took to the airwaves, the station created a ground system at its transmitter site, necessitating many kilometres of underground wire. As the story goes, Charlie Chamberlain donated his car to pull a plough, furrowing the ground so they could lay down the wire. Duke Nielsen, who had moved to P.E.I. by this time, was behind the wheel and, so says legend, put the pedal to the metal, leaving Chamberlain running behind him with the plough. It was likely a practical joke, and eventually Chamberlain and Rae Simmons finished up the job, Simmons being an on- and off-again employee of CFCY in various capacities, as well as playing the clarinet, or "licorice stick."

These efforts by Chamberlain, Nielsen, and Simmons were not for the sheer love of CFCY, though. They were also about making a living. Money was to remain an ongoing concern for all the Islanders. While as leader Messer always made more money, they all worked at non-music jobs in those years to make ends meet, from simonizing cars, in Chamberlain's case, to scraping tanks at Irving Oil, a part-time job that Messer held, according to his neighbours and friends, the MacLeans.

In the early 21st century some of the offspring of the Islanders would recall the financial worries of their parents, but they also remembered the good, ordinary times. Dawn (Messer) Attis remembered how she loved to pass the time with her Dad by sitting for hours on the doorstep of their P.E.I. home, or going fishing together. Ann-Marie Chamberlain (inspiration for Don Messer's composition *Ann Marie's Reel*) remembered the winters when her father, Charlie, would take the kids skating, making them hot chocolate upon return. Duke Nielsen's son Gary, who also became a musician, spent hours at his Dad's side helping him repair the bass which, due to its awkward size, constantly took a bruising.

Being kids, none of the Islanders' offspring seemed to think their dads were doing anything out of the ordinary at the time, and in some cases there was even mild embarrassment that their fathers didn't have "regular jobs." An understanding of just how special their musical fathers were would come later.

Back then though, older listeners already understood. The "Real Hoe-Down Specialists", as early 1940s write-ups sometimes called the band, gradually established themselves in their new island home as local celebrities. Once their popularity grew, CFCY's viewing gallery was frequently packed with fans standing three deep to catch a glimpse of Messer and the others in action. Those who didn't have the advantage of living in Charlottetown had to rely on much-anticipated opportunities to catch the band on tour.

One of the Best

During the summer months the Islanders began a tradition that was to become close to annual for most of their 34-year existence — the summer tour. Some tours lasted a few weeks, some almost the whole summer. In the early years they stuck close to the Maritimes. Later, from 1949 on, they toured to points west as well. It could be hard on the families of the band members, but from the start it was a necessary way to supplement their incomes, and a way to capitalize on some of the fame created by the CFCY broadcasts. In the early war years the tours were in conjunction with the war effort, and consequently the radio station tried to exert a certain amount of control over its musical representatives, issuing contracts governing the band's behaviour on at least two "good will tours" of the Maritimes.

The contracts, authorized by Art McDonald, laid down the law in no uncertain terms. Band members got their fees (either somewhere between $25 and $35 per week, or a one-sixth split after "necessary deductions for travelling") with the understanding that if "bad weather etc. interferes with tour" the amount might be "reduced by Mr. Messer." The men were instructed to practise "complete sobriety at all times," and failing to do so would require discharge by Messer, "without even consulting the station." There was to be no "bickering or arguing over salary settlements." In case that point wasn't clear enough, additional wording warned, "Any remarks such as used last year 'Is this all I get?' etc. will leave you open to discharge." There were also clauses guarding against fraternizing (or "entanglements") with the armed forces, and a reminder that "any attempt to 'take' women off soldiers or civilians" would be met with instant discharge.

It's safe to say that in the early days of the Islanders, life on the road wasn't without some issues.

Clearly McDonald was pleased with Messer's ability to organize the men, but anxious not to be cut out of the picture. A note on Messer's own signed contract of 1941 says: "As the tour was so splendidly conducted last year, we ask you this year for closer cooperation if possible, and a report on the men every two weeks."

McDonald's appreciation of the dedicated employee CFCY had in Messer was made obvious in a Christmas note that same year. "In the spirit of the day, and without any exaggeration it is splendid to be able to work with you every day," wrote McDonald. "There is no need of waiting until one is dead to say good things of them, so believe me when I say that you are one of the best."

Messer *was* one of the best, but so were the musicians who surrounded him. As the decade wore on the band coalesced, with the addition of Cecil "Cec" McEachern on guitar and violin, and Warren ("Warnie") MacRae on drums, two musicians who would stick with Messer to the end. The more consistent the line-up, the tighter the band got, and the more people loved to dance to the Islanders' music.

By 1942 the Islanders were crowd favourites — they had to turn dozens of people away at the door at performances such as the Milk for Britain Fair, held at the Peerless Clothing Co. Plant in Amherst, Nova Scotia. Twenty-five-hundred people came to the fair that night, breaking previous attendance records, and most wanted to get in to hear Messer and His Islanders. (Those unable to squeeze in had to make do with distractions such as Miss Zena Cheever, with her "many skilful [sic] and intricate dance numbers," as newspapers reported. As well, there were more serious presentations, such as displays of equipment used by the North Nova Scotia Highlanders.)

Also according to newspaper reports, L.A. McDonald, on behalf of CFCY, presented a donation of $25 to the Milk for Britain Fund. The fund, started by the Kinsmen Clubs of Canada in 1941, aimed to send huge quantities of powdered milk to deprived British school children, and it was just one of the efforts Canadians at home were making during the war years. There was no overseas conscription, at least, not until 1944's alteration of the National Resources Mobilization Act, when an Order in Council stated that 16,000 men could be dispatched. But Messer and most of his men (Duke Nielsen and Bill LeBlanc excepted) did not go overseas — otherwise the story of the Islanders would be a considerably different tale. Still, the effects of the war were felt in Prince Edward Island in numerous ways — and one way in particular had a direct impact on the band.

The influx of would-be flyers, training on P.E.I. as part of the British Commonwealth Air Training Plan (B.C.A.T.P.), created a jolt of youthful energy on the island. Initially the Charlottetown Airport was designated as the No. 5 Bombing and Gunnery School, but the B.C.A.T.P. met with some unexpected resistance — angry lobster fishermen. The intended bombing range would mean closing the lobster grounds on the North Shore. Needless to say, lobster fishermen were not pleased, and the expression of their displeasure was effective. Thus the base became the No. 31 General Reconnaissance School instead.

There were also aerodromes built on the island at Summerside, Mount Pleasant and Wellington. What this meant, among other things, was a population increase of young men from the allied nations, including dashing British airmen who liked to dance, even to the strange (to them) sounds of old-time fiddle music.

"Since the war began 'The Islanders' have had to curtail their pre-war personal appearance tours of the Maritimes, but they never refuse to play anywhere on request of the armed forces or the various service clubs who assist the war effort," ran one article in the summer of 1944, penned by Flo Fitzgerald, who referred to the band as a "popular and versatile organization." The Islanders had to be at least a little versatile to meet the dancing needs of the overseas contingent, more accustomed to ballroom and swing. But there was no getting around the fact that the heart of their music was still the old-time tunes, and it was simply not every airman's cup of tea.

Journalist Helen McNamara vividly described this reaction, writing post-war for the *Toronto Telegram* in 1949, in her column McNamara's Bandwagon.

"A lot of people don't care for the square dance music, the skirl of violins and chomp of an old-time piano. In fact, a lot of people have come right out and said they didn't care for Don Messer and His Islanders. But these same dissenters are chaps who had been brought up on swing bands and didn't know any better."

It wasn't just the overseas boys who were sometimes confounded by the sounds of the square dance tunes; at times it was Canada's own young men from "the far west and Ontario," according to McNamara. She interviewed once such doubter, Leading Aircraftman (LAC) MacGillicuddy, who put it succinctly: "We didn't care much for square dances ... we liked to shag in those days..." MacGillicuddy went on to say that "like the rest of the guys" he danced to the Islanders anyway, and although he recalled that "by the time I left the island I thought I'd be happy if I never heard a square dance again in my life," he also admitted, "... don't tell anyone but I'd like to hear *Rippling Water Jig* just once more."

What LAC MacGillicuddy failed to report, or perhaps didn't recall, was that the Islanders provided variety, surely one of the reasons they pleased even those who eschewed square dancing. There was always a certain amount of "modern music," at their war-time gigs, with Broadway tunes such as Gershwin's *Lady Be Good*, and there was also Duke Nielsen doing something with "coins, cards and rope," as one program from 1942 stated, plus novelty numbers including young women tap dancing. So if one didn't adore *Flop-Eared Mule* or the *Chicken Reel*, it wouldn't be a long wait for something more palatable.

It's difficult to imagine many of the young airmen were completely unmoved by the typical closing number though, a song that would become famously associated with Don Messer and His Islanders. In 1942, at a wartime performance in Summerside, P.E.I., it was noted on the rundown simply as *Smile Awhile*.

A Bigger Game

The popularity of the CFCY show ensured that it soon moved from daytime to evenings on Mondays, Wednesdays and Fridays, a prime spot on CBC's Trans-Canada network. Given their budding fame, Messer and His Islanders were considered a logical choice to bolster the flagging spirits of Maritime men and women in active services overseas. Consequently, in cooperation with the British Broadcasting Corporation, The Friendly Voice of the Maritimes was heard in a special wartime broadcast in early 1945, opening the program with a well-known favourite, *Lord MacDonald's Reel*. The broadcast was intended to bring "familiar music and news" from home. In the latter department, there was a range of subject matter, notably a heartstrings-tugging update on that other favourite Maritime pastime, hockey.

"Those who played Hockey and Foot-ball in the years before the war are now playing a bigger game," read the script. "It is true the boys under military age are still building their back lot hockey teams, and it is true also that they are showing a very great aptitude for the game, but most of the hockey that takes place in various ice forums is being played by Service Teams, comprised of men returned to Canada and by those who have not yet received their posting overseas."

After a passing mention of other winter sports, and the impending excitement of horse racing on the frozen Charlottetown harbor, the script quickly returned to its morale-boosting central thesis.

"For the thundering excitement of a real hockey game however, the Maritimes will wait for the return of the men of our former teams, and now 'Don Messer and His Islanders' bring you more recollections as they play *Souris Light House'*.

There was also an interesting observation made in the script, that there was "serious consideration" being given to the notion of building a bridge connecting Prince Edward Island to the mainland. Needless to say this consideration took a while yet — by the time Confederation Bridge was built in 1997 it was far too late to affect Don Messer's eventual decision to move to Halifax. Back in 1945 though, moving wasn't even a question. The Islanders were at home on the island, and they wrapped up their special war-time broadcast with a rendition of the *Operator's Reel*, followed by a hope that the overseas contingent would "be speedily and safely returned to Canada with the full knowledge of a complete victory over the forces of tyranny and oppression."

The Islanders provided a little leavening to thoughts of tyranny and oppression by keeping toes tapping throughout the war years, and into the post-war era of increasing prosperity. Life for musicians was still an ongoing struggle though, and that may be one of the reasons Charlie Chamberlain left the band in 1951, taking his family to Montreal for two years. But before his temporary departure there was an indelible change to the sound — and look — of the Islanders, with the arrival of a singer possessed of an extraordinary gift to touch the hearts of listeners across the country.

The Girl from the Singing Hills

A CBC Press Service release in one of the early years of her incumbency read, "Marg Osborne [sic] … is rather bashful and the boys enjoy embarrassing her."

Likely the boys in the band did indulge in a little harmless teasing of their one-and-only female band member in those early days. After all, when she joined the Islanders in 1947, she was only 20 years old, and most of the men were considerably older. Still, any teasing of Marg Osburne would be gentle at most, since from all accounts, in the entire quarter-century Marg Osburne sang with the Islanders, she behaved and was treated like a queen. A queen, that is, who knew humility, and truly had the common touch.

Marg Osburne wasn't the sort of person who would wish anyone ill, but it was a lucky break for her that Charlie Chamberlain was sidelined for a couple of months in 1947 following a car accident, since Messer brought in Osburne as a temporary sub. She was such a hit with audiences that when Chamberlain returned, she stayed on as well. If the man who was now nicknamed The Singing Islander had any concerns about being supplanted, those worries must have been swiftly put to rest, since the typically sentimental or spiritual duets sung by Osburne and Chamberlain (songs such as *Careless Hands*, or *Just A Closer Walk With Thee)*, were audience favourites. Osburne was the perfect performer for this material — she was anyone's idea of the nice lady next door, who just happened to sing on national radio shows. And Chamberlain was perfect as her slightly mischievous accomplice.

Unlike Messer, Chamberlain and Nielsen, Marg Osburne was not an especially early musical bloomer, although she was a fellow New Brunswicker, hailing from Moncton. But she hadn't imagined that singing could be a potential vocation until she found herself on the airwaves of Moncton's CKCW (after a visiting cousin bet she wouldn't audition). She did love to sing though, and had grown up singing with her family — folk songs, Stephen Foster tunes and hymns — learning harmony singing in the parlour and in the choir loft. Still, she had no ambitions of being a singer, so the success of her CKCW audition surprised her — really she had just tried out for a lark. The lark became a life though, and before she knew it she was singing regularly on the radio, sometimes billed as "The Girl from the Singing Hills."

It was inevitable, given the nature of the Maritimes, and of the intertwined communities of musicians everywhere, that Messer would eventually hear about Osburne. Some stories have it that he happened to catch her on the air, others suggest a CKCW employee forwarded a recording of one of her broadcasts. Whichever story is correct (and

Don Messer's Violin: Canada's Fiddle

Don Messer at 15 years of age on his family farm outside Tweedside, New Brunswick.
Notice the position of the fiddle. After his time in Boston you will see Don the violinist.

Don Messer's Violin: Canada's Fiddle

Young Don Messer with his first band in the Saint John, New Brunswick radio studio.
From left: James McCausland, Roy DuPlacey, Maunsell O'Neil (whose stage name was Joe LeBlanc), Eldon Rathburn, Don Messer.   Photo: Don Messer Estate, Nova Scotia Archives

Don's first band, first picture ever taken of the group in a radio station.
Maunsell O'Neil, Eldon Rathburn, Don Messer, James McCausland, Roy DuPlacey.
                                        Photo: Don Messer Estate, Nova Scotia Archives

Don Messer's Violin: Canada's Fiddle

Don and Naomi Messer.   Photo: Private Collection

The Original New Brunswick Lumberjacks. These three original members stayed together throughout their entire careers. Don Messer, Duke Nielsen, Charlie Chamberlain.

Photo: Canadian Broadcasting Corporation

Don Messer's Violin: Canada's Fiddle

The New Brunswick Lumberjacks prior to becoming "The Islanders".
Back row: Jim McCausland, Sammy Cohen, Duke Nielsen
Front row: Maunsell O'Neil, Don Messer, Eldon Rathburn, Ned Landry, Wally Walper

Photo: Don Messer Estate, Nova Scotia Archives

CFCY radio days.   Photo: Don Messer Estate, Nova Scotia Archives

Don Messer's Violin: Canada's Fiddle

The New Brunswick Lumberjacks:
Back row: Don Messer, Duke Nielsen, Charlie Chamberlain;
Front row: Ned Landry, Jiggy Watson.   Photo: Don Messer Estate, Nova Scotia Archives

Live "on air" radio show of Don Messer and his Islanders. Don Messer, Warren MacRae, Duke Nielsen, Marg Osburne, Harold MacCrae, Charlie Chamberlain, Rae Simmons, Jackie Doyle.
                                        Photo: Canadian Broadcasting Corporation

Don Messer's Violin: Canada's Fiddle

CBC Halifax Studio.   Photo: Canadian Broadcasting Corporation

CFCY Radio Days. Note the low position of Don's violin.

Photo: Canadian Broadcasting Corporation

Don Messer's Violin: Canada's Fiddle

Don Messer and Charlie Chamberlain in Charlottetown, Prince Edward Island (circa 1940).
Photo: Private Collection

The 1940s in Charlottetown, Prince Edward Island.
Rae Simmons, Jackie Doyle, Duke Nielsen, Charlie Chamberlain, Don Messer, Marg Osburne.
Photo: Don Messer Estate, Nova Scotia Archives

Don Messer's Violin: Canada's Fiddle

Don Messer, Duke Nielsen, Rae Simmons, Warren MacCrae, Harold MacRae, Marg Osburne, Charlie Chamberlain, Jackie Doyle.

Don Messer playing at the Halifax Hospital.

possibly both are), when Chamberlain went into the hospital and Messer was stuck for a fill-in, he remembered Marg Osburne with her strong voice, and sweet, lady-like presence.

Osburne's father accompanied her as chaperone to P.E.I., but he was soon satisfied that she was safe with Messer and the other fellows. Her Dad went back home to life in Moncton, expecting his daughter to move back home soon. She never did, though. Instead she became one of the Islanders.

On the Island

Being a capital "I" Islander resulted in a certain amount of fame, but it didn't follow that those born on P.E.I. felt the band members "from away" were necessarily bona fide natives. In 1971, long after their island years, a caller on a phone-in radio show in Halifax asked Don Messer how many of the band were "real islanders." Messer replied, in his soft-spoken, considered way, "A good representation I believe ... and I consider myself an islander myself — I lived there long enough."

Messer and the other transplanted New Brunswickers lived in P.E.I. for 19 years, long enough to raise families and have happy memories. Ann-Marie Chamberlain would recall that she greeted most mornings with three-part harmony, her Dad convincing his girls to do a little number en route to their cereal.

There were also some terribly sad times too, though. Don and Naomi Messer's youngest daughter, Brenda, who had been born on the island, died at the age of 18 months in 1944 from complications arising from whooping cough. Total strangers, fans of Messer's, wrote letters of condolence.

The public face of Don Messer was consistently one of quiet dignity; he was a man of so few words that any rift in his stoicism was rare. The private man was revealed only to those he was closest to, and this was the face his family saw in the nights leading up to Brenda's death, as he sat up rocking his ailing infant daughter. When she died, he was "terribly, terribly upset," as his eldest daughter Dawn would recall, remembering how her father came to meet her on her way home from school to break the awful news. Messer had always been protective of his daughters and was a worrier by nature; after the death of Brenda it seems he became more so. A year later, when Janis Messer was born, she became the child who had a more openly affectionate relationship with her father, and the one who was more protected, according to her sister Dawn. But Messer and his oldest daughter had a different kind of bond. "Dad always talked to me like I was an adult," Dawn recalled.

As the children of the Islanders were starting to grow up and the band marked its tenth anniversary on CFCY, they settled into a kind of groove. They had their radio show, Marg Osburne's calming presence, their assortment of part-time "day" jobs and the quiet life on the island. The line-up of the band was fairly stable, and there were modest tours with the core group in the early years of the new decade.

This early 1950s lull was accompanied by rumblings of big changes ahead though, changes anticipated by CFCY founder Keith Rogers. L.A. "Art" McDonald had died in 1950, and CFCY was going through a period of change, including efforts to expand its power by putting in a new antenna system. Rae Simmons did double duty at the station, playing with the Islanders and helping to operate the new transmitter site. But Keith Rogers had his sights set beyond the expansion of his radio station — they were trained on the new medium that would be nicknamed the "one-eyed monster," the "babble box," and eventually "the boob tube." In 1953, as the first sets made their way onto P.E.I., it was just called television.

The first P.E.I residents who owned television sets encountered one considerable problem with their newfound pride and joy — there was only intermittent reception from faraway stations. Keith Rogers wanted to be the solution to that problem, but sadly he died in 1954, before he could fulfill this dream. (The day of his funeral, crowds lined the streets of Charlottetown to celebrate their broadcasting pioneer. There had been a heavy snowfall the night before, but when Rogers' family got up in the morning, the steps and walkway in front of their house had already been cleared by a friend who had respected Rogers, one Charlie Chamberlain.) Ultimately, Rogers' passing did not mean the end of the CFCY television dream, just a delay. There were others who continued his work, and the television station went to air on July 1, 1956.

Earlier in the 1950s there had been few such major events in the lives of the Islanders. They did have a new band member though, the talented 21 year-old Waldo Munro, fresh out of a group called The Swingsters. There was also a small ripple of excitement in 1951 when Princess Elizabeth and Prince Philip were treated to a private square dance at Rideau Hall in Ottawa, where they were stepped out to tunes such as *Haste to the Wedding* and *Devil's Dream*, as well as *Don Messer's Breakdown*. (There was "no round dancing," reported the *Toronto Telegram*, "only squares.") The Princess was reported to have worn a brown checked blouse and blue flared skirt, and was said to have so enjoyed the closing number that she requested and received a recording of Don Messer and His Islanders to take home to England.

But for all that the first half of the 1950s were quiet years for the Islanders, they weren't without progress. Messer kept busy cultivating a following beyond the Maritimes, beginning with a first tour of Ontario in 1949, where audiences who had heard the group on radio were thrilled to see them in person. The Ontario fans were wildly enthusiastic, making CBC's decision in 1953 to move the show to a Maritimes-only broadcast seem a peculiar move. (In later years the CBC would boast of the band's radio popularity in Ontario in a press release describing the reaction of the police of Cobden, Ontario in 1952. Traffic in the town was tied up for three miles as fans flooded the roads in an attempt to hear the Islanders playing a hall designed for 600 people. According to the CBC release, nearly 6,000 people stood outside the hall hoping to get in.)

In 1953 though, for some reason CBC didn't get it — not, at least, until hundreds of letters of protest followed the absence of the Islanders radio show. The complaints came in from points west, causing the program to be reinstated in November, albeit in a weekly half-hour format. Regardless, the show flourished and, by 1954, the fan mail coming in to the CBC Press Services was mostly from Ontario, with Nova Scotia in second place. This time around, it was a relatively happy ending for Messer and the CBC.

Messer didn't do things by halves. He might have lost his thrice-weekly broadcast, but he and the band had their far-flung fan base, and he was determined to reap the benefits. In the summer of 1954 the band went on one of its most ambitious tours to date, beginning on the May 24th weekend in Scottstown, Quebec, and concluding on August 2nd in Nelson, British Columbia. Touring had its highs and lows, and out-and-out crazy moments. Duke Nielsen's son, Gary, later recalled an oft-told story of a drive through the Rockies, when the Islanders got out of the car to have a closer look at a bear. Presumably this was a well-fed black bear, not a grizzly, but in any event they played a practical joke on Nielsen, leaping back into the car and temporarily locking the doors, Rae Simmons shouting "wrestle him, Duke, wrestle him." Needless to say, they let their tame-circus-bear-wrestler cum bass player back into the car before any harm was done.

Over the years, stories of touring antics and mishaps became part of the lore of the Islanders, as well as the stuff of CBC press releases. In later, television-fame years, these releases often described an occasion at the Glace Bay Forum, when a coal miner was said to have "tapped a comrade on the head with a bottle," as the audience began engaging in more than mere fisticuffs with one another. On another occasion in Cape Breton the law apparently required the band to stop playing at one in the morning, but when they did, the evening ended with a "full-scale donnybrook."

Another, sadder story was of the square dance caller in Pilot Mound, Manitoba, who had petitioned Messer, as many did, to call the square dance portion of the Islanders' local performance. It was his dream, so the story goes, and his dream came true — except that he dropped dead of a heart attack at the end of the tune.

Such extremes aside, touring across the country was more often than not a grind, and by all indications not always hugely lucrative. Messer paid expenses up front, but no one got their share of the profits — if there were profits — until the end of the tour. Messer, as leader, took a considerably bigger cut, something that seems to have set some band members' teeth on edge. But as leader he assumed a greater responsibility, both in terms of having a musical vision, and in terms of running the business. In a 1955 agreement, Messer calling the shots meant he took 15 per cent of net profits; Charlie Chamberlain got five per cent, and the other men were down for two per cent. (In this agreement, Marg Osburne's cut is not mentioned at all.)

Messer set high standards for himself and the band musically, and he also tried to enforce a certain code of conduct. "Wives or sweethearts" were not allowed on these early tours (possibly because of space limitations and travel logistics), and if Messer was "dissatisfied with the conduct" of any of his band members, he could fire or suspend without notice or recourse.

All of this — the touring, the scrapping over small amounts of money — was stressful, and the stress began to show. The Islanders needed something to reinvigorate them, and that something was just around the corner. But before they made the turn, on the eve of their 1955 tour, Don Messer had the first of what was to be a series of heart attacks, reportedly while on the air during the radio show. He was forced to let the band proceed on tour without him, and according to oral history, the band was desolate. But not for long. Part-way through the tour a friend and neighbour, Cleaver MacLean, drove Messer to Regina where he could catch up with the others. Still, the heart attack was a big scare for Messer, likely setting him on a life-long path of anxiety about his own mortality. He was to clip and save newspaper articles on coronaries after the attack — including a 1956 piece in *The Star Weekly* which was accompanied by a photo of a man playing a tuba, captioned: "Living an active life after a heart attack does not extend to over-exertion like horn-blowing." Messer, fortunately, didn't play a wind instrument.

In 1956, health problems under control, the corner to new success was finally turned, when some Canadians got their first chance to see Don Messer and his violin up close on the small screen, as CFCY-TV began broadcasts from up on Strathgartney hill. Don Messer and His Islanders performed their first television shows there, hiking up the hill to the station, on snowy days dragging the big bass like a toboggan.

Messer was just biding his time though, probably with fingers crossed. Not for a regular show on the new CFCY-TV, but for something of a higher order, in terms of broadcast range and prestige. This hope was pinned on an event of the previous year, when the band had been interviewed and performed a few tunes on a show called *Gazette* at CBHT, the CBC Halifax television studios.

The show, hosted by Max Ferguson, was produced by an ambitious young man named Bill Langstroth who'd grown up with Messer's music in the early radio days, when Langstroth was just a kid living in Hampton, New Brunswick. Langstroth saw how the switchboard lit up following the group's *Gazette* appearance, and would later recall that the next morning he went into his boss' office and petitioned to produce a new show featuring Messer. His petition was a success, and the predecessor to *Don Messer's Jubilee — The Don Messer Show —* was born.

On November 4, 1956, CBC Press and Information issued an exuberant press release that read: "On November 16 at 7:30, the friendly face of Rae Simmons will lean towards a television camera and announce that this is… 'Don Messer and His Islanders.' In so doing, Rae will usher in the first of a series of 26 weekly half-hour television programs … The name, Don Messer, has become synonymous with the lively beat of hornpipes, jigs and reels."

Messer, as leader, was paid $100 dollars per show, negotiated with the CBC through the Halifax Musicians Association Local No. 571. Sidemen Nielsen, McEachern and drummer Gary McNevin each took home $50.75 (leaders were to be paid twice as much as sidemen according to union regulations), while Rae Simmons as steward received $65. Chamberlain, although listed as another sideman, negotiated $60.

The debut episode of the *Don Messer Show* opened and closed with two favourite fiddle tunes, noted on the rundown as *The Soldier's Joy* at the top, and at the bottom, *Big John McNeil.* Don Messer kept a copy of that rundown, neatly writing: "T.V.'s First Programs By The Islanders' " across the bottom.

The first program, but far and away from the last.

Chapter Three

"GOT MY DANCIN' BOOTS ON"

"Got My Dancin' Boots On, Got My Sunday Best..."

The jaunty tune was infectious, the perfect way to open a radio show and, as it turned out, a national television program as well. When *Don Messer's Jubilee* debuted on September 28, 1959, the *Goin' To The Barn Dance Tonight* theme was an invitation to a world of old-time music and values, hummed along to in living rooms across the country. If Charlie Chamberlain sometimes mischievously hooked his thumbs in his vest and sang "got my Sunday vest," instead of "best", or looked sideways at Marg Osburne as though he was debating whether or not to try and make her giggle, it was just another way of signalling to the audience, "folks, sit down, relax, this show is all about having a good time."

Messer and His Islanders had three years of television experience under their belts by the time the *Jubilee* debuted. They were stoked by the positive response of Maritimes television audiences, many of whom loved the "down to earth, toe tapping music," as they repeatedly told CBC switchboard operators. After the Islanders' first CBHT broadcast in 1956, almost 600 calls flooded the CBC switchboard, according to a CBC Press and Information release.

The national audiences had an advanced look at Messer and His Islanders as well, when *The Don Messer Show* was a summertime replacement for Friday night's *Country Hoedown* in August of 1959. Audiences across the country liked what they saw and heard, and they too were vocal about their reaction, to the CBC and to Messer directly. One viewer from Hamilton, Ontario joined the bevy of amateur poets across the land who would write poems to Messer over the years, typically paeans to the charms of the Islanders and their music. In this instance the ditty honoured the band's first outing as replacement for *Country Hoedown*, concluding with these optimistic lines:

"From coast to coast we'll watch for you each Friday.
So let those jigs and reels and breakdowns come our way.
Then the CBC will get so many letters
That the venerable board will raise your pay."

Messer also received mail from people in the "biz," such as Bobby Gimby, star of CBC radio's *The Happy Gang*. The "Pied Piper of Canada" (as Gimby was later nicknamed), wrote a congratulatory note to Messer after the network launch. He also enclosed a cheque for 15 dollars. The money was a gag, a response to journalist Gordon Sinclair's remarks in the *Toronto Daily Star* that Messer was "stinking up the TV network." Gimby suggested to Messer that ten-and-a-half dollars of the money should be used to cover the cost of 52 copies of the current issue of *Time* magazine, to be sent to Sinclair each week. The change was designated to purchase a large towel to "assist in wiping the egg off of his face."

Time magazine, it must be pointed out, held an opinion contrary to Sinclair's, labelling the show a "Hillbilly Hit." Messer would not have been partial to that headline, since he strongly objected to the music he played being called hillbilly, but he'd have had no arguments with the excellent publicity, let alone the sly barbs in Gimby's note.

Sinclair wasn't the only naysayer, though. Right from the start *Don Messer's Jubilee* provided a perfect target for cynical sniping, most of it from Upper Canada, or more specifically, from the city the rest of the country loved to hate: Toronto.

"It is one thing for Maritimers to be feted with their own hoedown delight," wrote a television critic in the Globe and Mail in September of 1959, "but it is something else again for the CBC to force feed the rest of the country with this corn."

Others, such as Ron Poulton writing for the *Toronto Telegram* later that autumn, took even fewer prisoners. "As a production piece, Messer's show makes me wince every time I look at it. It takes such studious care not to relax. Its props are museum pieces. Its bandstand looks like a refugee from a jitney dance."

Mind you, Poulton did admire the singer he called "Mary Osbourne, [sic]" saying her "bountiful frame and melodic style mark her as one of the very few new CBC personalities to emerge so far this year."

But the newspaper boys could grouse 'til the cows came home — it only seemed to make the fans even more devoted. They adored the show, and wrote lengthy letters to the editors of newspapers expressing their outrage when others dared to disagree. They seemed to like everything about Messer and His Islanders, and particularly appreciated the show as an antidote — the remedy for rock'n-roll. A typical fan comment of this kind in a 1960 edition of the *Telegram* read: "There must be many thousands other than myself who are heartily sick of the silly head flinging, finger snapping, knee waving so-called singers that flood the channels." This viewer went on to say that the negative remarks about Don Messer's music "practically border on heresy!" Many thousands agreed.

"No Stardust, They Were Just Folks"

When the Islanders were up for consideration for the 1959-1960 network television season, the CBC brass in Toronto apparently had some concerns about the presentation of the show. Perhaps by using a band member as MC the audience might mistake Rae Simmons for Messer, assuming the front man with the clarinet must also be the show's star. Plus, Simmons had an old-fashioned rapid-fire radio delivery, and it seems the powers-that-were wanted something more "with it." They found it in a handsome young CBC staff announcer named Don Tremaine, who had worked on the successful Halifax-based television program *Gazette*. Tremain was tickled to be asked to MC for Messer as part of his announcing duties. As he would recall years later, he first heard Messer on the radio when he was still "a little guy." Tremaine liked the music, and his mother's reaction to the show — she would always shake her head and say, "Boy that guy can really play the fiddle." So he was thrilled with the assignment, and later with the impact it had on his career — for years after the show was no longer on the air people would come up to him and ask,

"Say, weren't you Don Tremain?" He'd smile and agree. But mostly he liked announcing on the *Jubilee* because it was a pleasure working with Messer and company. As he put it, there was "no pretension, no stardust, they were just folks."

Simmons may have felt slighted, but there was certainly one advantage to being relieved of television hosting duties. He was able to focus on performing, and on musical face-offs with Messer, exchanges that charmed the audiences. Having Simmons full-time on music also meant the band grew even tighter. By the launch of the *Jubilee* the line-up was set, the group television audiences across the country would know and love for over a decade: Rae Simmons, Cec McEachern, Waldo Munro, Duke Nielsen, Warren MacRae and of course, Marg, Charlie and Don. There were other "regulars" on *Don Messer's Jubilee*, who in some cases stayed for years — organist Ray Calder, banjo man Vic Mullen, singer Catherine McKinnon, and the accordion-wielding Scottish singer Johnny Forrest, but the heart of the line-up was the eight people who rehearsed together, recorded together and travelled together. They were a kind of family, and as with most families, they were close and joking one minute, and in the next capable of driving each other slightly batty. Inevitably there were moments of resentment towards Messer, since he was the big boss and negotiator of the finances. But affection also kept them together, as well as something less tangible. That something was the vision of Don Messer.

The regional television years had given Messer a chance to shape this vision, based on his concept of variety. Gone were the magic tricks and fire-eating of live shows, but key to the concept was still "something for everyone." Every show featured guests, singers and dancers. There was always a varied palate of music, from exuberant fiddle tunes to the "quiet time," where Chamberlain and Osburne soothed with dignified hymns. In between, there was square dancing by The Buchta Dancers, an energetic, fetching young troupe choreographed by a Hungarian immigrant named Gunter Buchta.

When the Islanders performed live it was frequently to the sight of hundreds of twirling couples square dancing, and callers across the country dreamed of getting in with Messer.

Translating the excitement of the square dances to the tiny Halifax TV studio presented quite a challenge, though. Producer Bill Langstroth later estimated the studio was a mere 40 by 60 feet, hardly big enough for the musicians to find elbow room, let alone for a flock of dancers to do their footwork. Still, with clever camera work (on one occasion a diligent camera man ended up cornered by his own camera — the panning handle almost impaling him) and set design the studio appeared to audiences at home to be something like a parlour, where 19 or so people happened to sing, play music and dance.

Dancers such as Eddie Bourgeault stepped and tapped, sometimes to popular tunes along the lines of *Bei Mir Bist Du Shoen*, sometimes to Scottish and Irish tunes. Often there would be a few carefree steps from Charlie Chamberlain himself, twirling his trademark shillelagh. On rare occasion Don Messer proved he was more than capable of doing a little stepdancing as well, although he usually reserved this for a private audience. (Ruby and Cleaver MacLean, friends and neighbours from the Charlottetown days, would recall that after a scotch or two Messer, not much of a drinker, was more than happy to show off his step dancing talents in their kitchen.) For the most part though, Messer and his violin stayed in the visual back seat, playing the tunes his audiences loved so well, tunes he'd play over and over again. So often, in fact, that the violin had grooves on the fingerboard from repetitions of the fleet runs in *Rippling Water Jig*.

While the transition from radio to television was cause for great excitement among Messer fans, it wasn't the proverbial piece of cake for the Islanders, at least, not for Don Messer himself. For a natural ham like Chamberlain it was a different story, as he frequently confirmed to reporters. "The only difference I can see is that people are watching," he'd say, "But they've been watching us at barn dances for the last 29 years."

Of course there were other differences, just differences that apparently didn't faze Chamberlain. One was the concept of lip syncing. It soon became obvious that having the Islanders' audio performed live meant even more people and equipment had to be squished into the tiny studio, resulting in less control over every aspect of the production, from camera shots to lighting. Fortunately, early television audiences appeared not to be perturbed by the less-than-natural-looking consequences of lip syncing, nor by the supernatural effect of Marg Osburne harmonizing with herself, whilst miraculously no other singer appeared on camera as backup. (Langstroth would recall that some innocent listeners did write in asking why they never showed "that lady who sang along with Marg." Apparently these listeners accepted the explanation: "She's a secret.")

Chamberlain, a born entertainer, but one who had trouble recalling lyrics, may have actually found singing to pre-recorded music something of a blessing. A crew member standing to one side of the camera could hold cue-cards, or literally yell out the song lines in advance of Chamberlain's need to sing them.

For a private person like Messer though, television was intrusive in a whole new way. It was one thing to play in a radio studio where your audience, if there was one, was well separated by control room glass, or at dances where at the most folks wanted to shake your hand after the show. It was an entirely different matter to have a camera hulking towards you, ready to reveal your every facial twitch. Or, in the case of Messer in his early TV years, a profound difficulty remembering to smile. "After 25 years of radio you get used to a certain way of doing things," said Messer in one press release. "But when you know people are watching every move you make you have to worry about other things besides just playing a tune. I guess the word they use to describe television performing is 'demanding,' and that just about sums it up."

Messer had built a career around not shying away from "demanding," and television was no exception. In the earlier, pre-*Jubilee* shows Messer's nervousness was palpable; he barely hinted at a smile. But by 1959 he had mastered the modest smile that he could rustle up regularly throughout each show. That's as far as his obligation to the camera went; actually talking on camera was anathema to him. That's what

Tremain was there for. Messer's dislike of being front and centre confused fans at first, who couldn't understand why the star of the show didn't act like one.

"Which the hell is Don Messer?" wrote one viewer, tongue-in-cheek to Montreal Star columnist Pat Pearce. "Is he the fat guy who sang *A Rose Upon The Bible*, or the MC, or the guy who fiddles?"

For those who disliked the show, Messer's ambiguous role was irritating. "I caught only fleeting glimpses of Messer, and a good thing, too," wrote one Toronto viewer to the *Telegram*. "I was surprised to see that this Nova Scotian backwoodsman was the star of the show. He is obviously embarrassed at showing his talents."

Never mind that Messer wasn't from Nova Scotia, or that he'd spent most of his life living in small cities. The lines were drawn, and would continue to be drawn throughout the history of *Don Messer's Jubilee*. People either set their clocks by it, told their children to finish their homework in time to watch, or went to great lengths to be nowhere near a television set when it was on the air. Fortunately for Messer and His Islanders, an extraordinary number of people fell into the former camp.

The Number One Canadian Show

The advance program notes from CBC were at their most terse regarding the first national broadcast of *Don Messer's Jubilee*: "Music and dancing, country style, with the Islanders, singers Marg Osburne and Charlie Chamberlain and the Buchta Dancers." Following the broadcast, the log was a little more illuminating, acknowledging that guests on the debut show were fiddler Scottie Fitzgerald and dancer Harvey MacKinnon, and noting, among other things, that Marg Osburne sang *Bonaparte's Retreat*, and Charlie Chamberlain did the perennial favourite *With Me Shillelagh Under Me Arm*. Chamberlain and Osburne also sang a duet on what was to become a frequently requested number, *Whispering Hope*.

Other guests that first season included Don Messer's protégée, fiddler Graham Townsend, square dance caller Rod Linnell, singer Fred

McKenna, and Pipe Major Harold Sutherland, among a score of others, including folk music couple Peggy Seeger (famed folksinger Pete Seeger's half-sister) and Ewan McCall. These last two were an exception though, as they were not Canadian performers. Messer aimed to promote home-grown talent, and in a fairly even-handed way, which meant a steady stream of dancers, singers, small groups and fiddlers rotated through the show.

Messer's radio career had flourished in part because of an almost uncanny insight into what his audiences wanted, and his instincts for television proved no different. Proof was in the Bureau of Broadcast Measurement (BBM) ratings, released by CBC English programming on June 10, 1960. *Don Messer's Jubilee* was sitting pretty in the number one spot, reaching 1,706,900 households, ahead of the *Ed Sullivan Show* at 1,685,200, and far outstripping *NHL Hockey* at 1,539,400. The curmudgeonly anti-Messerite Gordon Sinclair took note. "You can blow me down," he wrote, "that Don Messer's Jubilee, the show that nobody wanted but the people, was the number one Canadian show during January."

One of the show's sponsors, Pillsbury Canada Ltd., took exception to this comment, as their marketing manager wrote to Messer: "He did make one slight omission," said the Pillsbury representative, "We feel it should have read ... the people and the sponsors."

The sponsors must have though they'd died and gone to heaven when they saw the ratings. Mind you, the first two sponsors of the *Jubilee*, Pillsbury (who boasted of baked goods made with "butter, *real* butter, between petal soft rolls"), and Massey-Ferguson Ltd. ("world's largest manufacturers of tractors with the one and only Ferguson system"), were heavy hitters in their respective markets and probably at least assumed a respectable return for their dollar. These sponsors appealed to two major Messer constituents — rural Canadians, and housewives. The latter (and likely Pillsbury too) could not know that during rehearsals some of the more devilish among the cast and crew would paraphrase Pillsbury's theme song, turning "Nothin' says lovin', like something from the oven, and

Pillsbury says it best," into the earthier, "Nothing says lovin' like a bun in the oven..." Those early days in the studio, saw some good times.

Don Messer's Jubilee was number one, but this didn't mean they were making first place money, or that the show was any big budget extravaganza. Exactly how much money Messer and His Islanders made from the *Jubilee* remains something of a mystery, clouded by a lack of existing documentation, and the complications of their multi-part incomes, generated from a combination of television, radio, recordings and live performances.

Knowlton Nash, in his book *The Microphone Wars: A History of Triumph and Betrayal at the CBC*, estimated that Messer himself never made more than $25,000 a year from his CBC income. According to the CBC itself, pay sheets and contracts for anyone connected with *Don Messer's Jubilee* do not exist — all records of financial transactions were destroyed, common practice at the time. Similarly the American Federation of Musicians (AFM) did not keep Messer's contracts. However, among Don Messer's personal papers there are two CBC contracts for the *Jubilee* years, one dated August 29, 1967, the other from February 18, 1969. Both are to engage Mr. Donald Messer's services as "Orchestra Leader," for *Don Messer's Jubilee*, in 1967 for the sum of $550 per occasion, for 13 occasions, and in 1969 for $650, for 11. There are no accompanying contracts for the band members (known as "sidemen" in AFM parlance), although according to AFM scale at the time, the minimum fee would have amounted to $61.64, for two two-hour rehearsals, plus two hours of overtime and an additional broadcast fee. Leaders, for the record, had to be paid a minimum of twice the amount the sidemen were paid, so it is possible Messer would also have received an AFM fee as well, topping up his arrangement with the CBC.

The difficulty in assessing this information is the lack of existing contracts for the sidemen. One would hope they were paid more than AFM scale, but, all things being equal in broadcasting and show business, one would be foolish to assume this was the case.

Interestingly, for those of a detailed turn of mind, in the mid-1980s CBC made an attempt to estimate what the performers on a number of original *Jubilee* broadcasts from 1963 and 1964 might have been paid. Messer, the CBC researchers estimated, would have earned $1,000 per show (clearly this figure is inflated, based on Messer's existing 1967 and 1969 contracts, even if there were additional AFM moneys), with Osburne and Chamberlain taking home $250 each, based on Alliance of Canadian Cinema, Television, and Radio Artists (ACTRA) contracts, the union governing singers. Oddly, there is no estimate for the rates paid to the sidemen.

As for the gross income derived from both television and touring, the reports were all over the map. *The Dartmouth Free Press*, for example, reported that Messer and His Islanders were in the "$100,000 class." But most accounts of the actual budget for the television show (including, presumably, producer fees and the like) indicate it was slight compared to other variety programs on both CBC television and elsewhere. Television historian Paul Rutherford, in his book *When Television Was Young: Primetime Canada 1952-1967*, stated that the 1968 budget for Don Messer's Jubilee was $8,000, "roughly one-quarter of the average for CBC variety shows."

Producer Bill Langstroth would later recall the last budget he signed off on was around $5,800, not far off from the estimate in a 1966 article in *The Telegram*, which reported the budget at $6,000. To add to the confusion, a 1967 feature in the *Atlantic Advocate Magazine* put the program cost at around $3,000 per show, acknowledging that "no one is too keen to talk about this." No one was; money was a touchy subject amongst the Islanders at the best of times. Yet in that same *Atlantic Advocate* article, Don Messer is quoted speaking about the bigger financial picture of the Islanders. "When we were in Charlottetown and on the road we were making gross about $80,000 a year. Last year we played only a month on the road, yet made between $60,000 to $70,000. Mind you, that has to be broken down amongst the entire cast. We are self-supporting in that we have to maintain ourselves and get no grants or anything like that. It's a business, you see."

It was a business, but clearly it wasn't a license to print money. Whatever the precise amount of money Messer and His Islanders did or didn't make from their various ventures, Messer was notoriously careful with his own income. The Depression mentality never died; he was frugal and resourceful. (Stories of Messer continuing to eat canned beans and Ritz crackers in his hotel room while on the road would continue to circulate many years later.) Messer, it seems, took what financial gains he had and did his best with them, investing in businesses, including the Canadian-owned "famous root beer" fast food kings, A&W. He never became a big spender though, always remembering those times he had tried to sell fish or coal door to door. As his daughter Dawn would say, he was the kind of guy "who never took too much food and always cleared his plate."

There was one overt sign of Don Messer's prosperity though, his brand new 1962 Thunderbird, the car that was his own personal benchmark of success. But in all other respects he remained his careful self — when his eldest daughter gave him a new stereo for Christmas to replace a decrepit kitchen radio, she found him moving the cast-off down to the basement for safe-keeping. (And, she would later speculate, because he really preferred the sound he got on the older radio). He didn't mind who knew that he lived simply, didn't hesitate to present a less-than-glamorous image to curious newspaper reporters looking for a scoop. Asked by a *Calgary Herald* reporter while on a tour in 1962 what he might be doing later that day, he was quoted as saying he had to go back to his motel room to wash his shirt. "I carry a box of soap flakes with me," he said. "Can't get laundry done while we're on tour."

Messer didn't drive the Thunderbird in the winter months, and he kept it in tip top shape. Sometimes he liked to just wander down to the garage and look at it, sitting there with its full tank of gas, as much as to say "Isn't that nice," admiring its shine.

On the strength of the success of the television show, and to avoid the frustrations of motoring to and from P.E.I., Messer had moved his family to Halifax in the late 1950s, and most of the other band members gradually followed. It was a difficult move for Don and Naomi Messer. They had made good friends on the island, and raised their family there, but the vagaries of weather and ferry crossings had become too much.

The Messer family settled in the suburb of Rockingham, and Don Messer's new-found "stardom" meant an equivalent new interest on behalf of the press. They began asking, "who is this quiet little guy with the violin, anyway?" Articles appeared extolling Messer's qualities on the domestic front ("hand Don Messer a violin or a dish towel — he's adept at both"), and describing his home (a "modern house … equipped with modern conveniences"). His preference in sandwiches was featured in a *Chatelaine* magazine article in 1964. (He enjoyed a club sandwich, bread lightly   toasted, and "heaps of green peppers on the side.") Messer's daughter Dawn, now a glamorous stewardess, was also the subject of mag-azine   features. His daughter Lorna was occupied with raising a family of her own, but Don and Naomi Messer still had their youngest daughter Janis in the family nest, and a younger boy named Gray, a relative's son, who lived with them for a number of years.

The other band members had growing families as well — in the first season of the show Marg Osburne gave birth to her second child, on March 27th, a daughter named Melody. Osburne was back on the air within a few diaper changes — appearing again on the *Jubilee* in early April. None of the group wanted to risk time away from their startling success story, unless, as was the case with Duke Nielsen, there was no choice. Nielsen and some of his family were in a brutal head-on car crash on Thanksgiving Day in 1961, and he was hospitalized for many months. In a CBC press release in December of 1962 Messer acknowledged, "It's been a tough struggle playing without him. He's been with us for more than 25 years and is not an easy man to replace." Ultimately Duke Nielsen wasn't replaced, and he returned to the program looking frail, and thanking the audience for their get-well letters.

"He Knew What Worked"

Don Messer's Jubilee was a testament to simplicity, drawing both the fire of critics who felt they should receive more sophisticated fare, and the accolades of fans who found the show an honest, refreshing delight. Regardless, the straight-forward format belied a considerable amount of forethought and pre-production. Most aspects of the show were masterminded by Messer himself. He chose the music and the guests, and wrote the arrangements for his band. In matters of camera angles, continuity, scripting and lighting, he worked with producer Bill Lanstroth (or temporary producers such as Jack O'Neil), who in turn consulted the lighting and camera crew, headed up by technical producer Rolf Blei. Messer and Langstroth both consulted closely with Gunter Buchta, choreographer of the Buchta Dancers. Buchta's own story was a tale in itself; he was at various times both a teacher and a lawyer, but following a World War Two injury that left him recuperating in a hospital for nine months, his physical therapy, dancing, led to an entirely new career as a dance teacher, first in Germany, and then in Canada.

Buchta's dance numbers were critical to the pacing of the show, and in his own way Gunter Buchta was something of a perfectionist — his "kids" were known as precision dancers, and were trained in ballroom as well as folk and square dancing. At their most athletic they were capable of doing startling Cossack-type leaps, but more often than not they sashayed, stepped or tapped in less dramatic fashion. Drama could be provided by the camera angle though, particularly shots from above, the square-dance skirts fanning out like flowers around the ever-twirling dancers.

If Messer was a product of the Depression, Buchta and his wife Irma, the group's costume designer, were products of immigration. They'd arrived in Halifax from Hungary around 1950, unable to speak English, but their drive to succeed in their adopted home was so strong that they soon formed their own successful school of dance, associated with the Maritime Conservatory of Music. Numerous troupes had auditioned to appear on *Don Messer's Jubilee*, but only one was deemed truly ready — and had the fringe benefit of a farm team of younger dancers always ready and eager to step in. The Buchta Dancers also could double as "greeters" at the live shows, circulating among the audience to sell souvenir programs or pictures of the band. Crew, dancers, cast — all in all television presented a much more complicated set of rehearsals and logistics. Messer met the demands though, or as Langstroth would later recall, "He knew his timing, he knew his programming from his radio days ... he knew what worked."

Something that worked best, in the entertainment business of the late 1950s, was of course television itself. It was over-shadowing radio, and Messer must have wondered if television meant his radio days were behind him. On September 26th, 1959, the Islanders broadcast what was intended to be their last CBC radio show. (Or, as the rundown for the show put it: "Almost 26 years and all happy years bringing our music to a wonderful audience across Canada.") Radio wasn't through with Messer though, as CBC press releases were to note in September of the following year. "Judging by the audience Messer's weekly program on the CBC-TV network draws," it read, "there are plenty of Canadians who like his brand of music." This was preamble to the launch of a new radio show, simply called *The Don Messer Show*, broadcast thrice weekly from Halifax on the CBC Trans-Canada radio network, beginning on October 3, 1960, and sponsored by Canada Packers. By December, the advertising agency that had negotiated that deal, Cockfield, Brown & Company Ltd., issued a press release headed "What An Audience!" saying that the results of a recent survey showed that "persons in one home out of every three tune in to the *Don Messer Show* on radio every week."

Cockfield, Brown and Co. also set up a radio promotion in early 1961 involving one of Canada Packers' products, "Domestic Pure Shortening," for listeners interested in obtaining a "long-play album" of Messer's, recorded specifically for the occasion, called *"Don Messer On The Air."* The shortening was pushed ad nauseam throughout the broadcasts, with Don Tremain, who also MC'd the radio show, charged

59

with some challenging segues: "It's surprising what interesting jewellery can be produced from the basic pieces available at any arts and crafts store," Tremain's script read. "All it takes is a little flair and imagination… the same flair and imagination you can use to create exciting baked goods when you have wonderful DOMESTIC PURE SHORTENING to help you." As for the recording itself, Tremaine's script introduced it thusly: "Here's exciting news for all Don Messer fans. The makers of satin-smooth DOMESTIC PURE SHORTENING have prevailed upon Don and the Islanders to record twelve of their all-time popular tunes… This new giant album features such hit tunes as *The Golden Wedding Reel, Jack The Sailor*, and *The Flanigan Polka*."

All you had to do to get the LP was to send in one dollar and fifty cents, along with the requisite box top, and presumably you could then listen to your Messer LP while enjoying freshly made "golden-perfect pastry and snappy cookies."

No matter how much they flogged though, sales of the "satin-smooth" stuff must not have met with the success Canada Packers dreamed of, since by 1963 McCormicks was sponsoring the radio broadcast, along with the Dairy Foods Service Bureau, and via a new advertising agency. Canada Packers' tenancy on Messer's show does have one lasting legacy though, likely collecting dust in attics across Canada — a recipe-card sized cookbook called *Baking for the Love of It*, its outer cover featuring a smiling Don Messer wearing a "Domestic" chef's hat, and a message from Messer himself: "I hope you'll enjoy 'Baking for the love of it' as much as I've enjoyed being 'chief taster'!"

But it was the *Jubilee*, not the radio show, that had fans in the palm of Messer's hand. Still, as the years passed he tried to maintain a connection to his first love, radio. In June of 1964 Messer marked 30 years of broadcasting by re-creating one of those early radio shows — on television. The Islanders travelled to Saint John for the broadcast, the city where Messer's career had started and, according to CBC press releases, re-created one of the radio shows, "using props, costumes, sets and original recordings from the 1930s." It's intriguing to imagine exactly what the original radio "costumes" might have been.

1964 was also the year that marked a second, albeit milder, heart attack for Don Messer. Supportive letters rolled in, wishing Messer a speedy recovery, from dignitaries such as MP Heath Macquarrie (a long-time Messer booster, who in 1960 had unsuccessfully petitioned Irish television pioneers to include the *Jubilee* on their fledgling roster) and Senator Gordon B. Isnor. There were also letters from friends and fans, including one signed "Bert" which read, "I feel that if the Don Messer show were to go on television without Don Messer it would be a completely meaningless affair … it would also make life much less bearable for me, and many others … Won't you please try to take it even <u>A LITTLE</u> easier?"

Messer did try. He stopped doing the radio show, despite the anxiety this caused him when fans in remote areas wrote complaining of the absence of their favourite program. Aided and abetted by his wife Naomi, he was more vigilant about diet and rest, although nothing, it seems, could ever stop him from his home-owner's habit of ruthlessly ripping dandelions from the Messer family lawn. It was against his nature to do anything by halves, whether it was lawns or television shows, and when it came to the latter the demands were relentless. There was just so much to do, and everything had to be done properly, or, as Messer felt, there was no point in doing it at all.

Big Eagle, A.K.A. Don Messer

Part of knowing "what worked," whether the end result was radio or television broadcasts, was having the right people on board — the right band members, the right crew and producer, and the right tour manager. Before the success of the *Jubilee*, Messer had used agents to help him book the band's tours, but none who literally went the extra mile by travelling with the band and easing some of the difficulties of logistics on the road. In 1956 he began working with a man who would — Ken Reynolds of Ottawa. Reynolds first introduced himself to Messer in 1952 when he was passing through Charlottetown with his client at the time, the singer Wilf Carter. Over the years their paths continued to cross, and eventually Messer, impressed by Reynolds' drive and keen sense of organization, hired him for the gig.

It wasn't full-time, since Messer didn't tour all year round, but when the band was on the road the load was tremendous, given that the full fleet of Buchta Dancers now accompanied the Islanders, and the press was clamouring for interviews. Plus Reynolds was intent on seizing all manner of publicity opportunities, including, for example, engineering a 1965 publicity stunt at the Banff "Indian Days," when Messer became "Chief Big Eagle," honorary blood brother of the Stoney Indian Tribe. This mark of respect involved the reportedly close-to-centenarian Chief Walking Buffalo inducting Messer into his new role, and Messer donning a feathered headdress, a photo-op if ever there was one. Messer, it should be pointed out, went on to compose a piece of music called the *Stoney Reel* out of respect for his newfound position. Messer's induction set a small trend, as in the following year Duke Nielsen was named a chief of the "Micmac Tribe," so the CBC's Information Services stated, for his outstanding contribution to the Red Cross as a blood donor. Could it really have been true that they named Nielsen "Chief Running Blood?" According to the CBC, it was so.

In the first half of the 1960s the success of the *Jubilee* translated into wildly receptive audiences in most places the band toured. They were frequently mobbed by fans, met by motorcades and feted with presentations and various honours and mementos. (In one instance, for example, the grateful inmates of a Saskatchewan penal institute presented Messer with a table lamp they'd made, in the shape of a prairie schooner.) The musicians found that performing benefits and making visits to senior citizens' homes, orphans' homes and hospitals was just part of life on the road, not always fun, but an essential aspect of the Islanders' wholesome image.

Some of their commercial performances were easy by contrast, although newsworthy in their own right. In 1960, for example, they performed at the Canadian National Exhibition as part of the Ontario Hydro-Electric Power Commission's unveiling of "The Arcade of Lights." Following a speech by Hydro's chairman, Premiere Leslie Frost was to flick a switch, turning on what was billed as "the world's most powerful lights," and then the Buchtas would begin to twirl as the Islanders played. Perhaps the chairman's speech went on too long, or perhaps the night-time crowds were well-lubricated and not afraid of voicing their displeasure. In any event, newspaper reports said that the officials were hurried off the stage as the audience "screamed" for the music to begin. One report said it was an indication that the crowd "preferred 'down east music' to official speeches, no matter how brief."

This was catnip to the *Jubilee*'s sponsors, and impetus, in the case of Massey-Ferguson, to sponsor a tour across the prairies in the spring of 1961. Cleverly combining a display of Massey-Ferguson's binders, combines and tractors with a chicken barbeque and performances by Messer and His Islanders, the turn-out for the show was phenomenal. Billed as "Farmarama" it was so popular that in its Saskatoon incarnation, traffic was terribly snarled, as somewhere between 17,000 and 18,000 people attempted to get into the show — allegedly a record number for attendance at any one building in Saskatchewan at one time. A Massey-Ferguson official, speaking to *The Star* said, "We had to chase people out of the arena after the show so he could put on a second show for those that could not get in." Not only was this stupendous publicity for Massey-Ferguson, it also had a direct, measurable impact, as according to the same spokesman, "… at the Ottawa show, a couple of months ago, our dealers took $170,000 worth of orders right on the floor. We think Messer's the hottest thing we've got."

Chubby Checker may have had a hit with *The Twist* that year, and Elvis Presley may have topped the charts with *Are You Lonesome Tonight*, but on the Canadian prairies, Don Messer was hot.

"The World of Tomorrow"

Although no-one back in Tweedside in 1909 would ever have dreamed it could be so, Don Messer was a boy born at the right time and in the right place. The Maritimes provided him with music that was viewed by many as being uniquely Canadian, albeit based on the "old time" music from the British Isles. Next, Messer came of age with radio, and radio provided the perfect new home for the music. By the time television emerged he had a tight-knit group of experienced entertainers who were able to successfully translate their act to the small screen.

The birth of television also coincided with a political and social climate that seemed amenable to Messer. When John Diefenbaker became Prime Minister in 1957, some CBC advocates were quaking in their boots, since before his tenure the new PM had been highly vocal about what he considered flagrant misuse of funds at the nation's station. It's true that once elected Diefenbaker paved the way for private broadcasters to have a greater status, and for public broadcasting to have a diminished role. But Diefenbaker, friend to the farmers, was also a supporter of Messer's; when CBC cancelled the *Jubilee* in 1969, Diefenbaker was one of the luminaries to speak out in protest.

While many Canadians were preoccupied with issues such as the move towards official bilingualism, the great flag debate (Union Jack vs. Canadian flag), or whether or not to use that new invention, the birth control pill, the Islanders were riding the crest of the wave journalists and advertising whiz-kids had long billed as "the world of tomorrow." It was a world perhaps best symbolized by television, vivid proof of post-war prosperity and progress. Few acknowledged that much of what was actually on the small screen was the visual equivalent of old wine in new bottles — the variety show, for instance, with its roots in vaudeville. For the CBC, variety shows also had a dual purpose — not only was their formula already in existence, and not only were they relatively simple to produce and immensely popular, they were also cash cows, a way to support more worthy, intellectual programming, because "the world of tomorrow" wasn't about the intelligentsia, it was about the average citizen. In 1953, about 10 per cent of Canadian households had television sets. In 1963, a mere decade later, the figure had jumped to 90 per cent.

Messer's success was an indication of something that some of the Canadian intellectual upper crust had dreaded all along, that television would fail to be a reflection of a more refined, "high art" version of Canadian culture. If the history of Canadian radio broadcasting had been shadowed by a struggle to define uniquely Canadian programming that the nation would support (as opposed to listening to, say, *Amos 'n' Andy* or Jack Benny), the development of television broadcasting aroused even more concerns for those intent on creating a "high-art" reflection of what it was to be Canadian, and to be in the arts. 1951's powerful Royal Commission on National Development in the Arts, Letters and Sciences (popularly called the Massey Commission, after its chairman, Vincent Massey) showed distant early warning of high anxiety about the potential for television to simply be one more far-reaching arm of the crassly commercial United States.

"Television in the United States is essentially a commercial enterprise, an advertising industry," read one section of the report, "Thus sponsors, endeavouring to 'give the majority of the people what they want,' frequently choose programs of inferior cultural standards, thinking to attract the greatest number of viewers." The Massey Commission had a tidy definition of culture as well, stating it was "that part of education which enriches the mind and refines the taste. It is the development of the intelligence through the arts, letters and sciences."

Don Messer and His Islanders were unlikely to be considered the sort of taste-refining art form the minds behind the Massey Commission imagined in their blueprint of Canadian culture. (Leaving aside the small irony that Vincent Massey was a Massey-Ferguson heir.) But people voted with their on-off dial, and for a time the mass appeal of a program such as *Don Messer's Jubilee* outweighed the slowly developing Massey-ized concept of Canadian culture. This concept ultimately belonged to the urban intelligentsia anyway, reflecting a split that was echoed by Messer's own audience throughout the *Jubilee* years — city versus country. It was estimated that at the height of the *Jubilee* the show reached 50 per cent of farm homes with televisions, as compared to 25 per cent in the city. That 50 per cent made their will known, since in the first half of the 1960s rural Canada (particularly rural Canada where citizens of Scottish and Irish ancestry were predominant) tuned in to *Don Messer's Jubilee* as regularly as they went to church.

Chapter Four

"THE PEOPLE'S CHOICE"

We Live What We Play

The amount of ink spilled over *Don Messer's Jubilee* was ample evidence of its dark-horse success. The scribblers of the land just couldn't quit scrutinizing its unexpected triumph. "What Makes The Don Messer Show Go?" read a *Chatelaine* magazine feature of 1961, expounding on how the television show "confounded show-business experts by making country corn Canada's favourite dish."

Messer, characteristically, liked to credit the success of the show to the music, specifically to the fiddle tunes he loved best to play, on his favourite violin. "The music is what carries us," he told the *Star* in 1960. "These songs have been around for two or three hundred years." But Messer was shrewd in his quiet way, and he, of course, knew there was more to it than that. "I believe it is because we are a crew of real people, singing and playing the music we like best for an audience who understands us," he said, speaking of the *Jubilee*'s success to a reporter from the *Saint John Telegraph Journal* in August, 1960. "Take Marg Osburne for instance. She may wear the same gown for several programs in succession. Women seeing this feel that Marg is just like them, no fashion plate but a real person and a real friend."

Or, as Messer put it on another occasion, speaking to yet another reporter, "We live what we play." His analysis was spot on. Fans were supremely unthreatened by Messer and company. After all, if the star of the show seemed too shy to even open his mouth to speak on camera, why wouldn't a viewer believe that these television folks were not so different from the folks at home? In a peculiar way, Messer's lack of "star" persona may have even contributed to the popularity of the show. One version of this assessment came from Bob Johnstone, writing in a much quoted *Star* article in August, 1960: "Messer talks, thinks, dresses and acts like a small town bank manager with a bookful of shaky customers."

Then there was the music. Fans of the *Jubilee* knew and understood the music that was performed on the show. And although few would dispute Messer's supremacy as a fiddler, there was something about the singing of Chamberlain and Osburne that seemed almost obtainable, making it possible for some viewers to think, 'If only I'd just practiced a little more when I was a kid, *I* might be up there with the Islanders too.' Columnist Jack Scott, writing about Chamberlain and Osburne for *The Sun* in Vancouver in October, 1960, put it this way: "They are not the world's best singers, but they are television's only genuine singers." Chamberlain, it should be pointed out, was an excellent singer, but by the time the television years rolled around he was not always in peak form. Still, he could always put across a song in a manner his fans loved. As for Osburne, she was innately musical, and had a much-admired purity of voice. Jack Scott's assessment was accurate — her real charm lay in that elusive quality of seeming "genuine."

To their fans, Messer and His Islanders also represented one idea of what it meant to be Canadian. A viewer from Toronto (there were some Cabbagetown residents among Messer's fans) described this concept clearly in a letter to the *Daily Star* in 1960.

"It is reassuring to see people with unashamed Canadian accents stand up without a shred of apology or pretence, or fear of sneers, and perform within their capacity in a manner that could only be a product of Canada."

It wasn't just the music that was Canadian. According to this viewer, it was also the step dancing, with its "peculiar straight-arm" style, cited as more proof of a popularity based on "a feeling of relief, mixed with rebellion and some pride." The relief and pride some felt on viewing *Don Messer's Jubilee* was not hard to understand, if the viewer in question had ancestry in the British Isles. The show was a weekly validation of the worth of the music and dance those ancestors had brought with them from the old country, and re-made in unique fashion on Canadian soil. As for the notion of "rebellion," if there was something to rebel against, it was the gradually changing face of Canada, characterized by shifting notions of cultural identification, and by the kind of music that would soon have young North America by the hems of their bellbottoms: rock'n-roll.

The "Canadian-ness" of the *Jubilee* provided ongoing fodder for many a columnist. Dennis Braithwaite, writing for the *Star* in 1960, suggested that at opposite ends of the spectrum, *Don Messer's Jubilee* and the program *Front Page Challenge* represented different facets of "the Canadian dream." In the case of the latter, it was a "reflection of a more up-to-date Canada, the image of a sharp, sophisticated, tough, knowing, and terribly modern Johnny Canuck who still manages to be a nice guy."

Messer and His Islanders, on the other hand, could settle for just being "nice guys." The same could not be said of those critical of the show.

"About as entertaining as a plowing match," said Jon Ruddy, writing for *The Telegram*, (the Toronto newspaper that loved to hate Messer) in 1960. In 1964, author Hugh Garner lavished paragraphs in a *Toronto Star* article over what he deemed "turgid" viewing, but he also felt obliged to be a tad more analytical than Ruddy. To his mind, the *Jubilee* was a retaliation against those superior Yankees, or, as he so pithily put it, "… it precisely appeals to the Canadian protester who flaunts his lack of sophistication vis-à-vis the U.S. by grinning through the gap in his teeth while spitting on the living-room rug."

Certainly by the 1960s the Islanders' fans tended towards an older, rural demographic, but this stereotype was nothing short of insulting. The *Toronto Star* put it more kindly (and accurately) in a feature in 1967: "They all come to the *Don Messer Jubilee* — the good people off the farm, the elderly men in plaid shirts, the silver-haired old ladies, the middle-aged men in windbreakers, the women in flowery dresses, and even the odd escapee from the go-go generation."

Garner's caricatured Messer fan must have appalled Don Messer, that down-to-earth gentleman with his tidy suits and slow glimmer of a smile. There was no question that the *Jubilee*'s audience was largely not university educated, and the show was not the stuff of sophisticated urban humour and wit, but equally true that simplicity was not a synonym for crudeness. One viewer held a very different view from Garner's of the *Jubilee*'s place in the artistic canon, expressed in a fan letter written in 1967.

"Don Messer, in music, puts together what Shakespeare did in literature, a balance of tragedy and of comedy..."

Perhaps announcer Don Tremain was to best sum up the success of Messer, and in somewhat less hyperbolic fashion:

"Don Messer," he said, "Was Mr. Ordinary with extraordinary talent."

"Full, Glorious Color!"

"Say, did you hear the one about the Halifax man who bought a colour television set and then returned it to the store when he discovered that Don Messer's Jubilee wasn't in color?"

The joke was making the rounds, circa 1967. But in March of that year the show finally began broadcasting in "full glorious color!" as *CBC Times* reported. "Imagine," the article continued, "The grey of Maestro Messer's hair, the bright tartan of the Islanders' jackets and Johnny Forrest's plaid and kilt, the multi-hues of the Buchta Dancers' costumes ... and even Charlie Chamberlain ... all in color."

By 1967 the Islanders' roles were firmly established: Messer the modest fiddler, Osburne the lady, Chamberlain the loveable clown, Nielsen with his alter ego Uncle Luke, and Simmons, MacCrae, McEachern and Munro the hardworking, affable musical accomplices. Banjo man Vic Mullen and singer Johnny Forrest were also regulars, but it was the original eight that long-time fans thought of first, when it came to *Don Messer's Jubilee*.

By this time there were also a couple of gossipy stereotypes perpetuated about Messer, and particularly about Chamberlain, that the former (being Scottish) was tight with money, and that the latter (a singer of Irish songs) drank too much. There would seem to have been elements of truth to both portrayals (Messer was very careful with his money, and Chamberlain enjoyed his rum), but also an unhealthy portion of fabrication and tall-tale telling.

Ken Reynolds, Messer's long-time tour manager, speaking 30-some years after Chamberlain's death, said that the stories about the man he described as "big loveable Chamberlain" drinking too much were "tremendously exaggerated," and "very hurtful." Chamberlain himself fueled the gossipy flames with his fondness for jokes about boozing, although it seems likely that kidding about the subject was at least partly his sly way of pulling the journalists' collective leg.

What is a certainty about Charlie Chamberlain is that he was possessed of a larger-than-life personality — he was a man of big appetites and great generosity. The stories of Chamberlain's kindnesses are legion, including one his children like to tell about the Christmas he gave away their Christmas tree (ornaments and all) to a neighbouring family who had no money. He made it up to his kids though, and according to his daughter Ann-Marie, they were proud of him for his act of kindness.

Chamberlain, along with Marg Osburne, was also as much a public face of the Islanders as was Messer. Ken Reynolds would frequently send Chamberlain and Osburne to do interviews or other publicity missions for the band, to take a bit of the pressure off of Messer, who disliked speaking in public, and the glad-handing that went along with being a star. And he was called upon to do a lot of both, as publicity for the *Jubilee* reached an all-time frenzy in 1967, Canada's Centennial year. On June 6 most of the television gang from the show began what was to be a series of live performances at 60-some centres across the country, celebrating Canada's 100th birthday. The Centennial tour started in Wabush, Labrador (although the official sendoff was in Halifax on June 10) and concluded towards the end of August with performances at Expo '67 in Montreal and the Canadian National Exhibition in Toronto. A weighty souvenir booklet (featuring Messer on the cover, surrounded by the provincial and territorial coats of arms) contained write-ups about the band members, and listed the tour's musical offerings — a well-loved assortment of polkas, reels, breakdowns and songs, concluding with the quiet time number, *God Walks These Hills With Me*. Reynolds was the mastermind; he'd schemed and plotted that this tour would happen with or without official government support.

It helped that John Fisher, the Centennial Commissioner, was (according to Reynolds) a fan of Messer's, but not everyone in the government ranks apparently felt the same. Reynolds felt that some people in government "were not inclined to think Don's show would fit in with what Canadians should have." This was likely true, since by the late 1960s, what many felt Canadians should have was "high art" — ballets, symphonies and the like. But when potential sponsors began writing hopeful inquiries about booking the Islanders on their Centennial tour (sent, at Reynolds suggestion, to the government's Festival Canada offices), the feds got on board, at least in name. Fisher, billed as "Mr. Canada," wrote a preface to the *Jubilee* souvenir booklet, concluding with the following: "In spreading the 'Maritimes Message' throughout Canada we feel that a deeper, more meaningful interpretation is being encouraged for our easternmost provinces. For a country continually striving towards unity, this is reason enough to wish the Islanders every success."

A bit lacking in specificity, but the underlying message seems to have been that the music of the east coast was still viewed as being distinctly Canadian, at least by some.

For the band, travelling mostly by bus with a few jumps by air, (to Whitehorse, for example), the tour was proof of one kind of unity that existed across the country — the unity of *Jubilee* fans. Most shows were sold out, and fans swarmed the band members to shake hands and get their programs signed. Reynolds recalled that on July 1, Dominion Day, they played an evening show in the town of Killarney, Manitoba. People started streaming in by late afternoon, and the arena was packed a solid two hours in advance. Being close to Turtle Mountain, the citizens of Killarney presented Messer with a live turtle. Messer, confounded by the reptilian, turned to Reynolds, whispering "What should I do?" and, following Reynolds suggestion, thanked the presenters for their kindness but suggested he'd be happy to return the turtle to its homeland, amidst much good humoured laughter.

The band and dancers must have been pleased with all the hoopla, but they must have also been exhausted — day after day they performed, went to bed, only to get up for an early start and a long bus ride to the next performance. They passed the time on the bus by playing cards, gabbing or catching up on sleep, and by missing their families. The stress sometimes showed, but no matter what, the *Jubilee* cast was almost never late for the early morning departures. Messer wouldn't put up with that. Besides, as Reynolds saw it, "No one wanted to let Don down."

After it was all over John Fisher wrote Ken Reynolds a long congratulatory letter, saying the Jubilee tour was "one of the most successful of all the Festival Canada attractions," and acknowledging the "tremendous amount of planning necessary to bring the show to so many places." As for Reynolds, the Centennial Tour was the crown jewel of his long-standing relationship with Messer, cementing his admiration for the man himself. "I thought the world of him," said Reynolds.

"Does Trouble Always Come in Threes?"

The Centennial Tour was built on the momentum of a series of themed *Jubilee* television shows the Islanders had broadcast over the winter months of 1967, musical salutes to the provinces and territories of Canada. (In fact the first show broadcast in colour was a salute to Saskatchewan, featuring *The Prince Albert Hornpipe*, *Cowboy Jock from Skye*, and *My Home in Saskatoon* among other appropriate tunes.) The work didn't stop after the tour though, at least not for Messer and Reynolds, who were strategizing about possible future successes. At the end of the Centennial year they jointly sent out the Centennial souvenir booklets to Members of Parliament, along with a Christmas message summing up the success of the coast to coast tour. As well, there was another agenda, one that had been on the back burner since 1965. The letter, signed by Don Messer on Ken Reynolds' stationary, slipped in a not-so-discreet hint about that long-term goal: "My personal wish, is to have our show televised in other countries. Perhaps through this media we could share our expression of the Canadian family, musical variety which has continued to be so well received. I hope we can count on your support to this end as well as a continuation of our weekly visits to your home."

Most of the MPs wrote back directly to Messer, congratulating and thanking him for his Centennial tour, as well as acknowledging his hopes for broadcasts beyond Canada. But the Honourable Pierre E. Trudeau, then Minister of Justice, had his private secretary respond to acknowledge receipt of Messer's letter and souvenir booklet. "He wishes me to assure you," the private secretary wrote, "that he has carefully noted the contents of your letter and will bear them in mind at an appropriate time."

Trudeau had other things on his mind than the fate of Don Messer, east-coast music, or a CBC television show featuring same. 1967 had been Trudeau's year, he'd influenced parliamentary reforms on abortion, divorce, and the rights of homosexuals, famously declaring "The state has no business in the bedrooms of the nation." On April 20, 1968, Pierre Elliot Trudeau became Canada's new Prime Minister.

Trudeau's Canada was a different creature than the Canada that had first welcomed *Don Messer's Jubilee* in 1959. Trudeau's predecessor, Lester B. Pearson, established the Royal Commission on Bilingualism and Biculturalism in 1963, and part of its legacy was the removal of some of the British symbols that had previously signified Canada (notably the flag and national anthem). Also, the social structures of the 1950s had shifted and were continuing to do so, with church attendance rapidly diminishing, divorce rising, and new ways of looking at the world — environmentalism, feminism, and a heightened awareness of bigotry and racism — headlined in news reports. Canadians were largely in the sidecar with most of these issues, watching the citizens of the United States struggling with civil rights and the Viet Nam war, while also absorbing U.S. popular culture. Television enabled Canadian viewers to keep abreast, and even if it did not reflect the day-to-day reality of one's own experience, there was a growing sense that American and Canadian culture were not so different.

In response to this there was the ongoing counter-trend towards a Canadian cultural identification focussing on "high art." The fruits of the Canada Council, established in 1957 as a result of recommendations by the Massey Commission, were borne in the form of funding to symphony orchestras, professional ballet and theatre companies and the like. It's true that in the Council's first year of existence they did grant folklorist Helen Creighton $10,000 to transcribe folk tunes, but this was the exception, not the rule. The funding of Canadian artistic life by the Council in those early days was largely the funding of "high art."

Meantime, the population of the country was shifting too, changes in Canadian immigration policy resulting in greater numbers of non-European immigrants. By the late 1960s the seeds were being sown for an official policy of multiculturalism, with its focus on more recent immigrant cultures, and a decided turn away from any notions of assimilation. The previously held "given," that the heritage of the British Isles largely defined what it was to be Canadian, was losing ground, in some eyes at least. And some of those eyes were at the CBC.

In 1967 the CBC's research department in Ottawa released a report on *Don Messer's Jubilee*, titled "*A Review Of The Program's Performance In The 1966-67 Season.*" Basing their findings on two primary sources, a panel of some 2000 respondents "selected on a probability basis to be representative of all persons in Canada, with television, over the age of 12..." and data from the A.C. Nielsen Company of Canada, the report represented the "writing on the wall" for Messer and company. The problem wasn't the ratings — 1967 Nielsen ratings showed the *Jubilee* was third in audience size for CBC-produced programming (after *Hockey Night* and *Flashback*, but ahead of *Tommy Hunter*) and eighth overall when U.S. programs were figured into the mix. True, the audiences were growing incrementally smaller, but equally true, as the study acknowledged, the show commanded "an abnormally high degree of audience loyalty." Interestingly, the themed Centennial broadcasts were "not quite as much enjoyed" by the audiences as the regular broadcasts of the season. While Messer could and did integrate music from various cultural strands into the program, the audience for the show was ultimately most interested in the old-time music, much of which reflected the heritage of the British Isles.

Where the study went for the jugular, was over the matter of what they described as the "Catherine McKinnon type." Singer Catherine McKinnon was young (20, when she joined the *Jubilee* in 1964) and pretty. Or, as a CBC Television press release described her the following year, "a pert 21-year-old who likes crazy clothes, zany sunglasses, odd-shaped furniture and the Beatles." McKinnon, also known as "The Nova Scotia Girl," represented something new, something that was much more about the folk music of the long haired sixties than the fiddle tunes of 18th century farmers.

Ironically, in the time period the report surveyed, McKinnon was no longer a regular performer on the *Jubilee*, and yet they included her when measuring audience enjoyment of regular performers, citing as their reason for doing so the fact that "she is still so well-known to 'Don Messer' viewers as an 'ex-regular' and as an occasional guest." This logic was specious; nonetheless, it enabled the authors to conclude that McKinnon's popularity, with the audiences who watched the program the least often and with those who least enjoyed it, was evidence of something amiss in *Don Messer's Jubilee*. This, along with a fairly detailed analysis of what various kinds of viewers — the faithful and the neophytes — liked and disliked about the show, led to the following summation:

"The implication of all this is fairly clear," read the report. "It is that those who are presently most attracted and those who are least attracted to 'Don Messer's Jubilee' have certain quite distinctive notions of how the program should be developed." (In other words, fans of the show held different opinions than people who weren't fans — not exactly a startling revelation.) Regular viewers, the report went on to say, were "satisfied with the character of the program … symbolized by the solid, earthy, old-time, no-nonsense performance of Don Messer himself." On the other hand, the viewers who least enjoyed the program, wanted "a performer of the Catherine McKinnon type."

Never mind that in one of the report's tables, measuring Audience Enjoyment Of *Don Messer's Jubilee*, 65 per cent of the viewers polled "enjoyed very much" the guest performance of Catherine McKinnon as compared to 67 per cent enjoyment of singer Tommy Common and step dancer Don Gilchrist, or 66 per cent of fiddler Johnny Mooring. Somehow this information could be ignored, and to some minds it apparently wasn't much of a hop, skip and a jump to the conclusion that the *Jubilee's* days, as a show promoting traditional east-coast music and dance, were numbered.

"Does trouble always come in threes?" began an article in the *Ottawa Journal*, written by Jim Bellshaw in 1968. He was referring to the health of three of the *Don Messer's Jubilee* stars. Osburne, who was recovering from eye surgery, Simmons, who'd injured a finger, and Messer himself, who had an operation for tendon damage in the little finger of his left hand — a violinist's nightmare. Around this time Messer was also diagnosed with diabetes, sending him on a path of renewed attention to diet, watched over by his protective wife, Naomi.

Trouble appeared to be coming in greater numbers than any mere trilogy for Messer though, most of it not highlighted in any public forum, beginning with that 1967 review of the program. In the early months of 1968, Ken Reynolds' petitions to the CBS, ABC and NBC television networks in the United States met with a distinct lack of interest. Then in the spring of that year, Messer was involved in an unpleasant legal dispute with the Progressive Conservative Party of New Brunswick, over their alleged failure to pay Messer and His Islanders for a performance at a Conservative party function. (One result of this was that the "New Brunswick Progressive Association, et al" were placed on the American

Federation of Musicians National Defaulters List.) To add to the legal wrangling, Messer was also engaged in arguing, through lawyers, over an agreement with Rodeo records which had come to a head early that year. Perhaps most unpleasant of all though was a conflict surfacing between Don Messer and the *Jubilee*'s producer, Bill Langstroth, over their differing views of banjo player Vic Mullen.

In a nutshell, Messer wanted to drop Mullen from the show. He didn't like his on-air presence (Mullen habitually grinned and winked at the camera), and he had concerns about his musical contributions as well. Langstroth, who had initially hired Mullen to appear on the show, felt otherwise. Speaking nearly four decades later Langstroth would recall the disagreement as the only dispute of any significance he and Messer had. It must have really rankled Messer though, since he tried (unsuccessfully) to part company with Langstroth earlier in the summer, petitioning S.R. Kennedy, CBC's Director for the Maritime Provinces. As Messer's side of the correspondence does not appear to exist, it is unclear whether his disgruntlement with Langstroth was mostly about Mullen, or if there were other issues as well — there's only Kennedy's response to go by.

"Although you may have criticisms to make about the way the program has been produced, you certainly can't argue with success," wrote Kennedy to Messer on July 10, 1968. "Under Mr. Langstroth's direction, the program has retained its enviable position in the national television ratings."

S.R. Kennedy turned out to be dead wrong about one thing. You could, as it turned out, argue with success. And, in the case of *Don Messer's Jubilee*, even win the argument.

Hoe-down on the Hill

In the eyes of fans, Messer was as Canadian as the nation's favourite sporting pastime, hockey. Or as one journalist put it back in March of 1963: "Pundits will ask what hockey players and Don Messer's fiddle do for unity. We think they unite Canadians in common interests and we like to parade before such Jeremiahs various French-speaking programs, bright and tuneful, that stubborn English-speaking Canadians have come to relish, becoming better Canadians in the process."

It's worth noting that for all that Messer was a symbol of anglo-Canada, and would have preferred Canada keep the Union Jack flying, he did include French-Canadian music in some of his programs, as this writer observed. As for hockey, 1967 had seen an expansion by the National Hockey League, one which favoured American applicants for new franchises over Canadians. In its own way, hockey was no more an undiluted symbol of what it was to be Canadian than was *Don Messer's Jubilee*.

Perhaps in response to the 1966-1967 CBC review of *Don Messer's Jubilee*, there was a new quasi-regular performer included on the show in 1968, the young country singer Myrna Lorrie, best known for touring with singer Hank Snow. ("Although not an official member of the Messer TV family," read a CBC Information Services press release just before the 1968 season began, "She can be called the show's 'adopted star.' ") By this time the *Jubilee* was the ninth most popular show on CBC television, fourth among Canadian produced programs, with an audience of 2,750,000. It was also in a new time slot, moved from Monday to Fridays, a change that Messer had not been happy about, since he felt Fridays were a less family-oriented viewing time than the old Monday evening slot. Still, the show must — and did — go on. But for how long?

It would not be an exaggeration to say that from the beginning, Don Messer saw the ending. He never took success for granted, and he never believed anything would last forever. Speaking to reporters in the heady early days of the *Jubilee*'s success, he was wont to err on the side of caution. Responding to a reporter from the *Saint John Telegram* he said: "How long will we last in television? That's a good question. We hope a long time, anyway, but whether we will stay at the top of the list is anyone's guess." Still, for all that Messer knew "all things must pass," it didn't stop him from worrying just what he and His Islanders would do once that day rolled around. As he told Bob Johnstone of the *Star* in 1960: "I don't know how long we'll be popular. We've been on the radio since

1934, coast-to-coast since 1939 on the CBC. But that doesn't mean people will like my sort of music forever. Musicians don't have any pension plans or things like that."

Messer remained a product of the Depression; anxiety about having enough money was never far from hand. It didn't help that the television show, one of his primary sources of income, offered about as much job security as a bed sheet in a blizzard offered warmth. *The Jubilee* was renewed on 11 and 13-week contracts, and that was that. The lack of security was clearly one of the driving forces behind Messer's determination to keep working as hard as he could, despite having had two heart attacks and, during the Centennial tour, a little "turn" which may have been a minor heart attack or perhaps just the result of stress. For Messer, stress was clearly not just from touring and being in the spotlight, it was also about potentially losing the spotlight. Producer Bill Langstroth would recall: "Every year for the last three seasons I'd had the feeling that this is not going to go on forever. I knew that Toronto wasn't going to allow it. I'd met enough of these people who had positions of trust, and decision making to do about programs, and I knew they really weren't in sympathy with anything but our ratings."

Despite Messer's own concerns over one day losing his program, it seems unlikely that when in February of 1969 he signed a contract with the CBC as Orchestra Leader for *Don Messer's Jubilee* for 11 more episodes, he would have believed it would be his last. Why should he? The program was still popular and the press was still exploring the mysteries of its success, as was evidenced in a column by Nancy White, later to become a singer-songwriter famed for witty songs, then a journalist writing for the *Dartmouth Free Press*. "It's very fashionable these days for reporters to visit the *Don Messer Show* and write smart witty stories about it and how, well, corny it is," White wrote, a few days before Messer signed that 1969 contract. "It's a fairly obvious target for merciless satire."

White went to a taping of the show herself, and then reported back. "Of course, you know what happened. I had a wonderful time, and came away thinking the show was the greatest invention since zippers, and that even if it's not your kind of music you have to admit that it's well done." White concluded: "So Don Messer's Jubilee remains basically the same as it has for years. It's still wildly successful and the congratulatory letters pour in."

Neither letters nor newspaper columns would stop the axe from falling though, and fall it did, first by telegram, on April 14, 1969, then by letter, both missives from the desk of Doug Nixon, then Director of Entertainment for CBC. The telex, sent to Keith Barry of CBC Halifax, pulled no punches:

"I HAVE NOW COME TO A FIRM CONCLUSION THAT A NECESSARY CHANGE IS THE CANCELLATION OF THE DON MESSER SERIES AND ITS REPLACEMENT IN THE OPENING SKED FOR THE FALL AND WINTER BY THE SINGALONG JUBILEE SERIES. THE REASONING FOR THIS IS TO INJECT A FRESH NEW ELEMENT INTO THE WINTERITME SKED AND PROVIDE A PRGM WITH A YOUNGER LOOK AND YOUNGER ORIENTATION. WHILE WE RECOGNIZE THE VALUES OF DON MESSER IN THE PAST WE FEEL QUITE DEFINITELY THAT THIS CHANGE WILL BE IN THE BEST INTEREST OF THE OVERALL SKED. WUD U PLSE SEND ME BY RETURN TELEX DON MESSERS HOME ADDRESS SO THAT I CAN WRITE HIM A PERSONAL LETTER."

Keith Barry must have telexed that address pronto, because Nixon did write Messer a personal letter dated the very next day, thanking him "on behalf of the Corporation for a very fine job over a long period." This time around, Nixon didn't mention anything about the replacement show, *Singalong Jubilee*, having "a younger look and younger orientation," instead he chalked the cancellation up to the need for change.

"Unfortunately, we must all look in broadcasting to elements of change and this has brought me this season to a choice of the 'Singalong Jubilee' Halifax series to replace your program," wrote Nixon, adding there might be occasions when "you and other members of your Company will do further shows for us," along with a final thank you for services rendered.

The CBC "sked" was never the same. And the audience for *Don Messer's Jubilee* let the world know exactly how they felt about that.

"He Felt Some Bad"

"Dear Sirs: Would you be kind enough to tell me what is the matter with the program *Don Messer's Jubilee*? I am well aware of the fact that it is a pity that we old people won't just drop dead and then you could get juveniles on all your programs and be happy, but could you really do better than the show to which you have given so much time in the past?"

"It's not that those who like country-western music from Halifax should be denied their pleasure, but wouldn't it be better to schedule the show on Saturday night — say at about 3 a.m.? What must people from other lands think when they check into a fancy hotel and turn on the CBC, about which they have heard glowing reports, only to see a program no other self-respecting network in the western world would run."

"I'm 23, not square, and must admit Don Messer is not my TV enjoyment. Rather, I found the words 'good riddance', coming into my mind when I heard it would be cancelled, but those letters in The Star made me realize that the young grow old, and someday I'll be in their position. Why must every media in our society cater to the wants and wishes of the younger generation?"

In the days following the cancellation of the show there was a "war of the letters" of which the above are three fairly representative examples, although by far the numbers of letters decrying the cancellation eclipsed the naysayers. If the press had lavished umpteen columns of ink over the years trying to fathom the success of *Don Messer's Jubilee*, some of the people of Canada expended at least as much passion debating the whys and wherefores of its cancellation. The precise number of thousands of letters of protest that poured into the CBC is not known, but as the days following the cancellation passed, the numbers continued to grow, newspapers

82

reporting 500 letters by the end of the first week following the news, 4,000 to 5,000 by the end of April. By early June, according to journalist Ernest Hillen, in a feature article for *Weekend Magazine*, the total number of letters of protest sent to the CBC was 7,500. By the end of that month, Pat Johnson, writing for *TV Weekly* would put the figure at 8,000 letters, and "1,500 irate phone calls." (The *TV Weekly* figures did not include some 400 petitions listing 11,000 names.) The show, Johnson also reported, had been number 11 of the top 20 Canadian shows a mere four months before its cancellation.

Even before the letters started amassing there was a newsworthy protest. On April 16, two days after the news of the cancellation broke, headlines such as "Hoedown on the Hill", popped up in newspapers across the country, as fiddlers, step and square dancers took to Parliament Hill on a rainy day in Ottawa. Curious onlookers watched and clapped as Don Gilchrist, a former *Jubilee* guest, proclaimed to the press that, "the intellectuals in Toronto are trying to destroy the last bit of Canadian folklore," before offering a lively sample of his own Canadian folklore talents. Gilchrist, also on the House of Commons maintenance staff at the time, spearheaded the hastily flung-together protest along with Messer fiddle acolyte Graham Townsend. Townsend took the unique stance of equating the protest with the American civil rights movement, according to a quote in the *Globe and Mail* on April 17. "The Negroes in the United States fight for their rights. We in Canada must fight for the Don Messer show," said Townsend.

French-Canadian step dancer Gilles Roy was quoted in the same article as saying he represented French Canada, particularly those in the Gaspé area "who will die if they lose Don Messer." The *Globe* also reported that politicians were involved, including MPs Jean-Thomas Richard (Liberal, Ottawa East) and Heath MacQuarrie (P.C., Hillsborough), offering their support of Messer to the crowd. After the protest, Halifax-East Hants MP Robert McCleave received permission for a second demonstration to be held on the hill a week later, and following that event he wrote to some of his fellow MPs, saying, "The Don Messer group worked like Trojans during the Centennial Year, and I for one resent the fact they were treated like dogs and learned of the non-renewal through a telegram from Toronto."

McCleave was tireless in his protestations of the cancellation. On April 14, when he had announced the termination of the program in the House of Commons (to cries of "shame") he declared he could "sense the flap of the wings of the culture vultures in Toronto," adding he wanted to "drive them back to their roost." On April 23, date of the second attempt to do just that from the hill, a crowd estimated at 300 shivered in the face of a bracing damp wind, listening to fiddlers playing reels, and holding placards, including a much-photographed poster saying, "Please Save Don," to which a fiddle had been strapped. Meantime, in the Maritimes both the Prince Edward Island and Nova Scotia legislatures passed resolutions seeking further consideration from the CBC, and Premier Louis Robichaud of New Brunswick wrote directly to George Davidson, President of the CBC. Like the protests on the hill, the Nova Scotia resolution was offered in the musical spirit of *Don Messer's Jubilee* — Benoit Robichaud, the PC member from Yarmouth, playing a reel on his fiddle as members returned from recess.

Perhaps the most noteworthy voice of protest from a politician was from former Prime Minister John Diefenbaker, MP for Prince Albert, widely quoted as charging the government with finding out "why so popular a show as Don Messer's is being cancelled." MP Barnett Danson (Liberal North York) suggested to the house, in a wise-cracking moment, that "Messer fiddle while the member for Prince Albert burns."

The campaign to reinstate Messer stormed on for weeks, with ads placed in Halifax's *Chronicle Herald* saying "Like the Don Messer show? Then why fiddle around ... leave the fiddling to Messer and you — join the protest!" And a 35-foot telegram from Fort William Ontario was forwarded to the constituents' MPs. Then, later in April, Ed Schreyer (NDP-Selkirk) was quoted as suggesting that the performers from

Don Messer's Jubilee should take part in the celebration of the new National Arts Centre in Ottawa. The two-week long celebrations were reported to be running a deficit, and Messer, suggested Schreyer (presumably cognizant of the delicious irony), could help the government defray this financial burden and "give Ottawa high society a lift."

Of course the press had plenty to say about the cancellation as well, some of it speculating as to the underlying issues that contributed to the *Jubilee*'s demise. Television critic L. Millen of the *Globe and Mail* wrote on April 22, 1969 that "the CBC has talked nervously about appealing to younger audiences and similar guff, without getting into such basic reasons as the fact that the show had been around for so long that people at network headquarters here were getting sick of it. This is a period in CBC history when large structural changes in the network's hierarchy are taking place and no one wants to be thought of as in any way old-fashioned."

Millen, not a fan of Messer's ("Personally I would sooner open a vein with a rusty fork than even watch another Don Messer Jubilee") also saw the cancellation as a strike against what in CBC parlance would be termed "the regions", particularly the region of the Maritimes. "Historically, there has also been a network antipathy to things produced outside Toronto, and if Messer's people had been here instead of Halifax, the show might have survived along with such venerabilia as *Front Page Challenge*."

The CBC suffered another embarrassing moment when *The Globe and Mail* reported on April 24 that the local CBC station in Ottawa accidentally ran an old Messer promo, one which said, "Television is Don Messer's Jubilee, that's what television is all about." According to the *Globe and Mail*, a CBC spokesperson said, "Someone must have been asleep at the switch."

All the furor was ultimately for nought though, since on May 1, 1969, State Secretary Gerard Pelletier told the Commons that the CBC was "sticking to its decision to cancel the Don Messer Jubilee show."

How, one might well ask, did Don Messer take all of this? His response to Doug Nixon, the CBC's messenger, was dated April 23, 1969, and was typically polite, but also typically not without a dart or two. "I am sure by now you realize your mistake," Messer wrote, "In changing our programme for that of 'Singalong Jubilee'…While I know that the decision will not be reversed, it does give me a great deal of satisfaction and gratitude to learn that we have had so many supporters." Messer, careful to keep the door open for future work concluded, "Should there be a change in your plans, I might say that I am always interested."

Singalong Jubilee, a summer replacement show since 1961, now had the dubious distinction of replacing *Messer's Jubilee* during the regular season. It was hosted by Messer's producer, Bill Langstroth. To call this an awkward situation would be quite an understatement. Langstroth would later say that he was unhappy about the way the cancellation was handled by the corporation, and that it was a moment in his career when he felt "inadequate," and "kind of dumb about the whole thing." Naturally enough though he looked forward to hosting his own show, but it was a horrible way for his long association with Messer to end. In early May he sent a letter to Messer. "I find it most difficult to summarize in a few words my total feeling about our truly wonderful association on DON MESSER'S JUBILEE," he wrote, going on to recall some of the favourite moments he'd shared with Messer over the years.

Doug Nixon, meanwhile, must have been sweating at least a little bit under the glare of all the negative publicity. However, according to Knowlton Nash in his book *The Microphone Wars*, Nixon had been and remained determined to get the show off the air.

"I am bloody well going to kill the geriatric fiddlers," Nash quoted Nixon as saying to a colleague.

By autumn of 1969 Nixon must have been heartily sick of the letters he was still forced to send out to viewers carping about the cancellation, and hoping the decision would still somehow miraculously be rescinded. "I regret having to tell you that his program will not be back on our network this year," wrote Nixon to a disgruntled viewer. "However,

Don Messer's Violin: Canada's Fiddle

Don Messer, at CFCY. Photo: Don Messer Estate, Nova Scotia Archives

Waldo Munro, Rae Simmons, Marg Osburne, Cec McEachern, Warren MacCrae, Duke Nielsen, Don Messer, Charlie Chamberlain.

Photo: Canadian Broadcasting Corporation

Don Messer's Violin: Canada's Fiddle

Don Messer, the radio days.   Photo: Canadian Broadcasting Corporation

Don Messer and his Islanders, 1956. First year on regional television, CBC Halifax Studio.
Rae Simmons, Cec McEachern, Don Messer, Ray Calder, Charlie Chamberlain, Gerry McNeil,
Duke Nielsen.   Photo: Canadian Broadcasting Corporation

Don Messer's Violin: Canada's Fiddle

Don Messer, Catherine McKinnon (frequent program guest), Charlie Chamberlain, Marg Osburne.
Photo: Canadian Broadcasting Corporation

Back row: Cec McEachern, Rae Simmons, Gary McNeil, Marg Osburne, Waldo Munro
Front row: Duke Nielsen, Don Messer, Charlie Chamberlain.

Photo: Private Collection

Marg Osburne.   Photo: Private

Charlie Chamberlain.   Photo: Don Messer Estate, Nova Scotia

Don Messer's Violin: Canada's Fiddle

Marg Osburne, Charlie Chamberlain.

Charlie Chamberlain, Marg Osburne.

Don Messer's Violin: Canada's Fiddle

Gunter Buchta, explaining his choreography for the Buchta Dancers before a *Don Messer Jubilee* taping in the Halifax CBC Studio.   Photo: Don Messer Estate, Nova Scotia

Charlie Chamberlain on set in the Halifax CBC Studio.

Photo: Canadian Broadcasting Corporation

Don Messer's Violin: Canada's Fiddle

Gunter and Irma Buchta. Irma made the costumes for the Buchta Dancers.

Photo: Don Messer Estate, Nova Scotia Archives

A later picture from *Don Messer's Jubilee*, with Johnny Forrest (accordianist and singer, fifth from the left) and television host Don Tremain (eighth from the right).

Photo: Canadian Broadcasting Corporation

Frank Leahy with Ed Minevich collaborating on their show "Bending the Bows".

Photo: Private Collection

The Don Messer Show, is being produced by a Hamilton station and is available for purchase by local stations in Canada. Perhaps you could influence your local station to buy it."

Well, it was one way of doing business.

With all of the fuss and emotional upheaval, the cast and crew somehow managed to finish the final tapings that May. Ernest Hillen, writer for *Weekend Magazine*, reported on the taping of the last show, step by heart-wrenching step. The performers, cast and crew were subdued, Messer and the men dressed neatly in light grey suits, red ties, with matching handkerchiefs. But when it came time for the show, there were plenty of jokes and laughs during the station breaks — after all, they were performers. Bill Campbell, a former camera man on the program, was there in a wheelchair to watch the final show being put to bed, and he told Hillen that the music helped him imagine he could do a little dancing himself.

After they finished the show there was a party at the CBC for the complete cast and crew, and later that night a smaller private party for Messer at guitarist Cec McEachern's house, this one in honour of Messer's birthday the next day. According to Hillen, at midnight the band presented Messer with a new violin case, bearing a plaque that read "To Don on his 60th from the Islanders," as they all sang "Happy Birthday."

But when the last notes of audio had sounded at the taping earlier that evening, Bill Campbell was wheeled out of the studio weeping. And 36 years later, piano player Waldo Munro would remember Don Messer's personal reaction to the end of the *Jubilee*.

"He felt some bad, I know that."

"By Golly, That's a Cracker"

Life went on, immediately and with a vengeance. In June, Don Messer and His Islanders departed on what was billed as the Farewell Tour, Messer telling the press his touring days were done. He'd been touring since 1949 and he was 60, after all. (Although, as Charlie Chamberlain was quoted quipping to a reporter from the *Cornwall Standard-Freeholder*,

"There's many a good tune in an old fiddle, you know.") Messer never entirely stopped touring, he just scaled back, doing small tours and one-off live performances. And in the wake of the cancellation, Don Messer and His Islanders were usually billed as "The People's Choice."

Naturally reporters were curious to know Messer's feelings about the cancellation. In most instances he was quoted as saying, with typical restraint, only how disappointed he was with the way the news was handed down. Sometimes he got a little more pointed though. "I would have liked to get together with the directors and president," he was quoted in the *Halifax Chronicle Herald* as saying. "[CBC President] Davidson was here last week, he should have had the courtesy to call... I had planned to retire in two years in a graceful manner. It was a rather underhanded way to get the notice."

That was what really smarted — the lack of proper respect. Messer knew that the program, like all radio and television shows, would inevitably end. And perhaps he even knew that the show, compared to its early years, was showing signs of age — there wasn't quite as much verve as when the Islanders first came into the living rooms of the nation. Still, when enterprising independent broadcaster CHCH of Hamilton, Ontario came calling, promising to syndicate the show, Messer seized the day. By the end of May, newspapers were reporting that come August, Messer and His Islanders, along with the Buchta Dancers, would be taping a series of 26 shows in Hamilton, for broadcast over the course of the fall and winter. They were to be produced by Manny Pittson, a freelancer who was, ironically, also the producer of CBC's *Singalong Jubilee*.

Pittson was a pioneer of shooting musical performances on location (years later famed Canadian television innovator Moses Znaimer would call Pittson the "father of all music video") and a fan of Messer's. Pittson would later remember Messer's initial reaction to the idea of coming to Hamilton.

"It wasn't terribly hospitable at first, it was cold, he would give me nothing in writing. He wasn't hostile, it was cautious — after 40 years in the business you should be cautious."

But Messer soon agreed. As for the folks at CHCH, they saw getting Messer as "the second coming," as Pittson put it, and twenty-some stations across the country apparently felt the same. In June of 1969, the Halifax station that picked up the show, CJCH, published an article in its in-house journal saying, "Welcome home Don! The CBC isn't buying Don Messer's country-hall brand of fiddlin'... but we are!"

Pittson didn't mess with the *Jubilee*'s well established formula, ("I wouldn't touch a damn thing," he said later); the biggest change being a new MC, Sandy Hoyt. Pittson respected Messer too much, saying "he had an unfailing instinct for what was right and wrong, for him and for his band and for his viewers." The production schedule was compacted into five or six weeks, and some of the press following Messer's every move made much of what appeared to be a grueling schedule for a crew of aging musicians. Messer, interestingly, said on a private radio station interview in 1971 (promoting the launch of the NFB film *Don Messer, His Land His Music*), that the schedule actually suited him. "It's a good way to do the programs, I enjoy working this way. There's no lost time, and you get through it and the job's done."

Messer did take a pay cut to come to Hamilton, signing agreements with Pittson for $400 per program (again, likely in addition to the musicians' union scale), but no one could put a value on the satisfaction he must have felt at having another broadcaster jump all over the opportunity to air the show. Pittson believed Messer also accepted the CHCH offer to ensure the band members and dancers still had gainful employment. ("He did it for the troops.") Pittson couldn't say whether or not the CBC cancellation had left Messer demoralized, though — Messer played it too close to the vest for that. Regardless, Messer still loved the music, appreciating it when the band nailed a tune. "By golly, that's a cracker," he'd say.

Don Messer's Jubilee ran for four seasons on CHCH, and in the first Bureau of Broadcast Measurement ratings of the show, in March of 1970, it ranked number one in ten of those 20-some markets. There were plenty of people, it seemed, who still liked to hear the band play *Ally Crocker*, or hear Marg Osburne singing *Sweet Memories*, Johnny Forrest with *The Road To Dundee*, or Charlie Chamberlain with his perennial Irish numbers, *Dear Old Donegal*, or *Galway Bay*.

CHCH was a face-saver, and it created a certain amount of continued profile and income for Messer and His Islanders, but not to the extent that the CBC had. During the CHCH years, Messer began casting about for other opportunities as well. Among his papers from the 1970s are a number of letters exploring the possibility of returning to his first love, radio. There is a tone of, not desperation, but anxiety in those letters, as though the ignominy of being deposed from the nation's station was motivation to achieve even greater recognition elsewhere. Finally, in 1972, Messer had his touring agent, Ken Reynolds, write on his behalf to CBC television about the prospects of a return to their airwaves.

Thom Benson, Doug Nixon's successor at CBC television, responded sympathetically to the query, acknowledging what he was already on record as saying, which was that he had felt the *Jubilee* cancellation was ill-advised. But he could not offer Messer a new show.

"Since the cancellation of the Don Messer Show," Benson wrote, "We have been developing 'Country' type shows which have filled a void left by what I felt to be a premature move." Benson didn't mention *Singalong Jubilee*, the show that had replaced Messer, instead he wrote about another program, *Countrytime*, one that he felt was well established. This probably galled Messer, since the musical director of *Countrytime* was none other than banjo player Vic Mullen. More importantly, it indicated Messer's unstoppable determination. For all his talk of retirement, he clearly was continuing to seek fresh opportunity, no matter what. However life, and death, would not allow it.

In June of 1972 Charlie Chamberlain collapsed with what was reportedly a combination of a heart condition and lung congestion, following a show rehearsal in Hamilton. In July he went home to the Maritimes to recuperate, and on July 16, 1972, he passed away. Newspaper reports said that more than 500 friends and admirers packed the church for his funeral in Belldune, New Brunswick. Although Don Messer was listed (along with some of the other Islanders) as an honorary pallbearer, the gang was not at his funeral. They were still in Hamilton, in the midst of their compressed CHCH taping schedule, all the performers having flown to Hamilton to tape every episode of the upcoming season. Still, it sounded a strange and sad note in memory of Chamberlain that they did not attend the funeral. However, producer Manny Pittson felt Messer's decision was based on a complicated set of emotions.

"He didn't go to the funeral because A, I think he was in denial. B, I think he was afraid of his own health. He never asked anybody if he could go or not, he just said we're not going, no, we can't do it ... The show goes on." Pittson didn't feel this meant that Messer wasn't upset about Chamberlain's death — to the contrary. "He held it in pretty good though, but you could tell by the hunch of his shoulders." In the weeks leading up to Chamberlain's collapse Messer, recalled Pittson, would not admit that Chamberlain was unwell. "He'll go on forever," Pittson remembered Messer saying.

Sometime in the following year a reporter from the Saint John's *Evening Times-Globe* asked Messer about the singer Tommy Common, who had filled in for Chamberlain, and was likely to sing in his stead during the upcoming 1973-1974 television season. "Not to replace Charlie," Messer said to the journalist, "No one could do that."

But there was no next season. On March 26, 1973, Don Messer died in Halifax, of a heart attack. He was 63. His funeral service was in Halifax's Calvin Presbyterian Church, filled to capacity, with another hundred or so mourners standing outside. Ruby MacLean, Naomi Messer's good friend, would later recall that Naomi told her, when Don died, "part of her died with him."

***

Speaking to the *Calgary Herald* in June, 1962, Don Messer was quoted as saying: "I don't feel a person should ever retire. You should maintain an interest in life. If you give up, you don't usually live too long. I guess we'll never quit. We'll just fade away."

They didn't fade away though, and as for Don Messer — he never quit.

Chapter Five

DON MESSER'S VOLIN: CANADA'S FIDDLE

A Good Instrument Needs to Be Played

Don Messer's eldest daughter, Dawn, looked up at the violin in the top of her closet, where it had been sitting for over two decades. She was preparing to move, to a small cottage in the countryside near Halifax, and was faced with making decisions about what she would take — would she move the violin, simply to store it on another shelf? Looking at the case, with its plaque wishing her famous father a happy 60th birthday, she could almost hear his voice saying, "a good instrument needs to be played."

It wasn't the first time the words had echoed in her mind — after all, her Dad said them often enough when he was alive — but now it was nearly a quarter of a century since he had passed away, and keeping the violin as a memento began to seem more and more senseless. She would never, after all, forget the man who was her Dad — he was "a wonderful father," she would say.

When Dawn's mother, Naomi Messer, died a few years after her husband, Dawn and her sisters carried on as inheritors of their father's extraordinary legacy of music, recordings … and violins. None of the three were musical, and yet they had grown up steeped in the sounds of the Islanders, and hearing their Dad playing the violin.

Following their mother's death, the Messer girls had to decide what to do, not just with *the* violin, but also the dozen or so other instruments that were in his collection. They agreed to split them up between the three of them, and Dawn, as eldest, got first choice. She immediately chose the violin her father had played through all those years of radio and television shows and barn dances and parties, the French violin with its big sound, the sound that just floated into the air when Messer played it.

Now 25 years later, the violin's strings were decaying; its bridge was all but falling over. But what was the point of repairing the instrument if it wasn't to be played? The time, Dawn decided, had finally come. But the question remained, who should play Don Messer's violin?

Ask musician Frank Leahy the same thing, and he will tell you that every fiddle player in Canada should have a chance to play Messer's violin. He sees the instrument as a symbol of the country, as a living emblem of a significant part of Canada's history. And through sheer happenstance, he came to be the guardian of Don Messer's violin. Sheer happenstance, that is, if you believe it was a total coincidence that Leahy, then in his 30s, decided he wanted to record the *Jubilee*'s theme song, *Goin' To The Barn Dance Tonight*. And because he planned to do an updated version of the music, he wanted to get permission from Don Messer's estate. It was for this reason he first contacted Dawn (Messer) Attis, right around the same time she was puzzling over what to do with her father's violin.

Gretzky to Lemieux

Frank Leahy didn't want to be a musician, when he was a small boy in Teeswater, Ontario. Back then he dreamed of being a hockey player. But his doctor father, Phil Leahy, was also a fiddler, (as was his grandfather), and from the time Frank was four years old he played the violin, his Dad giving him lessons and making sure he practised. Leahy grew up listening to his father's record collection, which included recordings by Fritz Kreisler, Stephane Grappelli, and Don Messer. There were two pictures hanging in the kitchen that told you what was what in the Leahy household: a framed photo of the Pope, and right beside it, one of Don Messer. Knowing this, it should come as no surprise that one day Frank Leahy would decide to spend a year in the seminary, nor that when studying for two university degrees (one in science and one in music) he would pay for his university tuition by playing the violin.

The science degree from the University of Guelph came first, (all the while playing the fiddle … and varsity hockey), with the final year of his studies coinciding with his first-place victory at the prestigious Canadian Open Old Time Fiddle contest in 1984. Even after this honour Leahy still didn't believe he'd make his living by playing music, so after graduating (and a year in the seminary), he put his science degree to work, through a job as a pharmaceuticals salesman. All the while his father continued to believe his talented son should take a serious crack at music as a full-time pursuit, and in the late 1980s he persuaded him to return to university to get a music degree — Frank Leahy's trip to Boston, if you will.

Leahy began to study with one of Canada's best, Eduard Minevich, a violinist who had been soloist and concertmaster of the Leningrad Concert Orchestra before emigrating to Canada in 1975. As well, he started part-time studies at Wilfrid Laurier University's music program in Waterloo, Ontario, and studying privately with Minevich, then concertmaster of the Kitchener-Waterloo Symphony Orchestra. At the same time he continued working for the pharmaceutical company — and raising a family of what would eventually be seven children. It wasn't casy, to say the least, but Leahy, possessed of a tenacity not unlike Don Messer's own, persevered, and after graduation he came up with an idea that was to be successful literally beyond his wildest imaginings. It sprang from a growing interest in an unexplored musical meeting point, the intersection of classical violin and folk styles — in other words, fiddling. He approached Eduard Minevich to see if he would be interested in representing the former style, and Minevich, who had a history of "symphony pops" performances, agreed. The two performers created a number of groundbreaking shows that drew new audiences to symphony orchestra concerts, including *Road to Carnegie Hall*, *Master Clash*, and most notably, a show called *Bending the Bows*, a spirited treatment of the encounter between a classical violinist and a fiddler.

This show became so successful that eventually Leahy and Minevich dropped most of their other work, and toured across North America for about four-and-a-half years. But Leahy did manage to squeeze in the occasional extracurricular professional activity, including the recording project where he decided he wanted to do an updated version of Messer's famous theme song.

From the first time they spoke, Dawn (Messer) Attis was curious about Frank Leahy. About his career, his family, about what he thought of the music industry and other fiddlers. Leahy, an affable, chatty guy (his nickname in college was "Happy") was a bit taken aback that Messer's daughter took such an interest, but he accepted it without undue questioning. He had no reason to think twice, after all, since at the time he didn't know that Don Messer's violin was still extant, and he certainly never imagined Don Messer's daughter was essentially vetting him as the potential keeper of the flame. Then one day she finally came out and asked him: "Do you want to have my Dad's violin?" For Leahy, it was a moment like no other, he "just couldn't believe it." In later years he would compare it to another, very different moment, similar only in its shock of happy good tidings.

"It felt like when I watched the '87 Canada Cup when Gretzky passed the puck to Lemieux and he put it in the top shelf. It was overtime, it was a fantastic goal, it was perfect."

When Frank Leahy told his family that he was going to play Don Messer's violin, his father wept.

Canada's Fiddle

It was late at night one evening in 1997, when Frank Leahy finally took Don Messer's violin out of its case. He hadn't shepherded the violin home from Halifax himself, since he was in the middle of a series of performances on the west coast, so his parents had travelled on his behalf to get the instrument — Dawn (Messer) Attis would not allow it to be shipped. An undisclosed sum of money had changed hands, but a more significant transaction was yet to come, a musical transaction between the violin and its audience.

But that first night Leahy was alone with the violin. He waited until his wife Lisa and their kids were in bed, and the house was quiet. Then he went into his music studio, and began to play. He would later recall the experience as being "very eerie," as though the living history of the instrument was palpable. It was as if, he said, the spirit of the violin was an old house where many people had lived, and had lived happily. And in his mind's eye, he could see the face of Charlie Chamberlain, grinning from ear to ear.

It wasn't long before he was playing the violin in front of crowds, and witnessing its startling effect on listeners, the violin invariably acting as an intense trigger of memories. At every one of these performances there would be people "bawling their eyes out," Leahy would recall, as soon as they heard Don Messer's violin playing some of the old tunes. This reaction convinced him that there must be some other way he could share the instrument, but it took time to discover what that way might be. Then, before a performance in Elliot Lake, Ontario, an old man approached him saying he was a fiddler hoping to get a close-up look at Don Messer's violin. Leahy spontaneously asked him if he'd like to do more than look — would he like to play a tune? The man, shocked and thrilled, picked up the instrument and began to play. When he finished playing, he too started to cry.

Later, at the end of that evening's show, Leahy invited the man to play the tune again from the stage, and the crowd just loved it. The light bulb went on. This was one way to share what Leahy had begun to think of as "Canada's fiddle" — to let people take their turn with the bow. Now fiddlers sometimes line up by the dozen at the end of a Leahy concert, waiting their turn to play a tune.

"The power of Don Messer's violin is amazing," Leahy has said. "It's beyond imagination the way it affects people."

Tucked under Leahy's arm, as the violin was once tucked under Messer's, it began to travel the country, once again making history after its long confinement. On one occasion, on the coast of British Columbia, Leahy and his partner Ed Minevich received an invitation to fly in to the Hartley Bay reserve, south of Prince Rupert. They jumped at the chance to visit the isolated community, even though it meant taking a small four-seater plane — and Leahy was not a fan of flying. Part way there the weather turned bad, very bad — moving from rain to sleet to snow, the winds buffeting the small plane around like it was a rubber ball. Leahy thought he was a goner, and with every new updraft he found himself wondering if the case for Don Messer's violin was waterproof, and could he swim to shore if he landed in the drink? Fortunately Leahy didn't have to test the buoyancy of the violin, let alone his own swimming abilities, and they made it to land, safe and sound.

In a fitting conclusion to this particular voyage, the next day an elder on the reserve took Leahy aside to show him the tree under which she had been married, decades before. The reason? When she got married, back in the 1940s, she and her husband didn't have any money, and they only had one 78 record to play after the ceremony, a recording of Don Messer playing *Rippling Water Jig*, which they played over and over while people danced. In an emotional moment, Frank Leahy played the tune for her once again, on Messer's violin, underneath the same tree.

To Leahy, the violin's impact on people is matched only by the impact Messer had on fiddling itself.

"He established the base mark of fiddling — no one else has reached that level. There are other great players, but he's like Donovan Bailey, he holds the record, and in Messer's case the record hasn't been broken."

Mr. Messer's Music

You won't find "old-time music" between Old Hundred(th) and Old Roman Chant in the *Harvard Dictionary of Music*. In fact, you won't find any precise definition of the term at all. In Canada, (unlike the United States, where old-time typically indicates music developed in isolated rural areas of the Appalachian mountains), old-time most often refers to the traditional fiddle tunes themselves, particularly those tunes that arrived on Canada's east coast in the late 1700s. However, some would say that Canadian old-time music also includes Victorian parlour songs, sacred songs, songs from minstrelsy and British and American ballads, with fiddling as just one branch on the old-time family tree.

As a term it came into popular use by the 1920s, via record companies capitalizing on music that they could now record and sell for the first time. In Messer's day people seemed to just "get" what old-time meant, it had a certain quality, or, as L.A. "Art" Macdonald once said on a CFCY radio show introduction to the *Alley Crocker Reel*: "Here's something real old fashioned, low down and close to the floor."

Ned Landry, who played harmonica and fiddle in some of Messer's earliest groups, viewed the music as having a special power to move people in the opposite direction from the floor, or as he put it in the year 2005: "Well, I say old-time music's like medicine, just like that. I mean there's something about it. It just gets them up dancing!"

Old-time has also been used as a synonym for "down east" music, which in turn became synonymous, at one time, with the music that Don Messer played. Of course old-time was already old-time when Messer was a young man, which isn't to say that his first radio audiences necessarily understood that. A script from one of the very early Messer radio shows, hosted by an unknown voice, ran as follows: "Before turning the microphone over to Mansell [sic] O'Neil, I want to say a few words about the popular conductor of the *New Brunswick Breakdown* — Donald Messer. Don is not a middle-aged man as many of his listeners believe — he is still in his early twenties and deserves a great deal of credit for his ability as an old time fiddler."

What made old-time music self-consciously "old-time" — and part of the reason for Messer's enormous impact on the genre — was the advent of recorded 78s, radio, and eventually television. Messer recorded prolifically, around thirty-five 78s for Apex, and around 30 LPs (some reissues) for Apex, Rodeo and MCA. He also put together a number of popular song books, featuring tunes he liked to play and including some of his own compositions. And if a fiddler had a recording of Messer's, he'd likely listen to it over and over again, and it was equally likely he'd imitate

Messer's style. This was a quantum leap from past methods of learning the tunes, when most fiddlers learned them live, from another player, without that point of reference to return to again and again.

In Messer's early career, some also used the term "old-time" as a synonym for "hillbilly music," a term promoted by the recording industry as well, and a term that Messer disliked. He viewed hillbilly fiddling as something from the southern U.S., where, as he told Pierre Berton in an interview, the fiddler would "saw away on maybe two strings." As for his music, usually he would say, as he did in the *CBC Times* on his 30th anniversary in broadcasting, "It's not Western or cowboy music. Our tunes have been around for two or three hundred years. They're folk tunes passed down from generation to generation, and many of our listeners remember hearing them in their homes and at community gatherings as youngsters."

When it came to the media, more often than not reporters were less interested in the music itself, than in the intangibles (why was his television show so popular?) or in misguided human interest stories (aren't Charlie Chamberlain and Marg Osburne married in real life?). Still, once in a while some music-minded journalist would pop the question, or something close to it. "What is down east music?" asked Ron Sudlow in the *Victoria Daily Times* in 1963. "It's the old ballads and tunes of our ancestors," Messer was quoted as responding. "Western swing is the old tunes with more variations around the melody. The down east music has more melody and those little swingy licks added." In other words, to Messer's mind down-east, old-time, call it what you will, signified the old tunes from the old country, played pretty much the same way for decades, but with "little swingy licks" dressing them up just a bit.

A more easily solved conundrum is the age-old question of what makes a violin different from a fiddle. In fact there is no difference, at least not as far as the instrument itself is concerned. There is, however, a difference of perceived values, one which has shifted over time. It's interesting that Messer, who did sometimes refer to the instrument as the "fiddle", often preferred to call it a violin. Perhaps it was the legacy of his Boston years, when he learned to hold the instrument as a classical player would, under the chin, not against the inside of the shoulder, and to read and write music. (He was a "note reader" as some old-time fiddlers would say.) It's likely that "violin" sounded more dignified to him, and being a person who played the violin also distinguished him from those players who could play only by ear. Certainly Messer prided himself on his musical literacy. As quoted by writer Lester B. Sellick in the late 1960s he said, "Without a knowledge of music I couldn't have done it. I really got it from the lessons — from the scales and the arpeggios based on those scales. Right now I feel that I can get the melody from any violin score no matter how difficult it may look. What I'm after is the melody — everything's a melody." Messer went on to observe that by playing second and third violin parts, which he considered more difficult than first, he learned to "watch the time exactly," all of which would stand him in remarkable stead in later years.

The fact that Messer sometimes drew attention to his formal training on the violin, as opposed to the fiddle, may have also been an attempt (conscious or otherwise) to try to distinguish himself from some of the competition, in those early days. After all, in 1928 Manitoba-born George Wade, with his group the Cornhuskers, and their popular three fiddle sound, already were meeting with considerable success on the radio.

But whatever Messer did or didn't think of the instrument he played, there was no question as to the function of the music that was played on it. The raison d'être of those old fiddle tunes was to accompany dancing, and nobody did that better than Messer and His Islanders. (It's equally true that among the innovations Messer can be at least partly credited with, is the notion that fiddling could also serve as more — as accompaniment to singing.)

When the band played live they didn't just stick to old-time though, they mixed it in with "modern music" which usually meant contemporary dance music — waltzes and fox trots, but also a smattering of jazz and Tin

Pan Alley tunes, sometimes filtered through the big American swing band sound. This explains something of the Islanders' innovative instrumentation — Rae Simmons' clarinet, for example. How many old-time bands had a clarinet player, or a pianist and bassist who could also double on trombones? Not so many, although there was something of a parallel with an American movement of music called western swing, a hybrid of country and jazz. Don Messer was certainly familiar with that music, as the recordings of Bob Wills and his Texas Playboys in his record collection attest.

"Modern music" was an important ingredient in the Islanders' shows. (And in even earlier incarnations of Don Messer's bands — in the early 1930s he had a short-lived ensemble charmingly called Don Messer and His Modern Men.) "Modern music" was a way of getting a different segment of the crowd on their feet. ("For all you younger fans who like a bit of jitterbugging," MC Rae Simmons would call out to the audience, before the band launched into something with a little bit of New Orleans or swing feel to it.) Messer was able to pull off the modern music in no small part because of the talents of his band members, particularly Duke Nielsen, who had played briefly with Benny Goodman, and Simmons, who knew how to execute "hot" licks, and Waldo Munro, who had thoroughly absorbed the stride of Fats Waller. Messer liked that about Munro's playing, telling him, "never let the right hand outshine the left." It's a fact that most of this "modern music" was never recorded by Messer though, more's the pity.

Don Messer's television show was of course weighted to the old-time, but it too had a broader scope; there were the piano features for Munro, a range of song-types from Osburne, Chamberlain and the guest singers, as well as the closing hymn, and the Buchta Dancers taking care of the do-se-dos. Ultimately though, while Don Messer no doubt pondered the sources of the music he played, he wasn't nearly as concerned with defining what the music should or shouldn't be called, as he was with creating a blend that he just knew would satisfy the people at home.

Fiddle-obilia

The late George A. Proctor, a musicologist with the National Museum of Canada, once wrote that "old-time fiddling is by far the most important type of instrumental folk music in Canada." If you dropped the words "old-time" from the equation the statement would still ring true. Canadian fiddling remains a strong, living tradition, albeit a difficult one to parse. The styles (with their distinct methods of bowing, ornamentation, and in some cases repertoire) are as subtly diverse as the country itself, and include Cape Breton, Ukrainian, French-Canadian, Acadian, Ottawa Valley, Métis, Newfoundland and more. Many of these styles have also mutated and shifted as players have borrowed and shared their music. Messer, in his own extensive record collection, had some of the earliest recordings ever made by Canadian fiddlers, including Cape Breton performers such as Winston "Scotty" Fitzgerald and Angus Chisholm, and French Canadians J.O. LaMadeleine and Joseph Allard, among hundreds of other fiddle recordings he collected over the years.

As recording formats became more accessible — and easily mailed — Messer also exchanged tapes of fiddle music with fiddlers he met while on tour, and for years he had been actively sharing some of his transcriptions. (His daughter Dawn would remember how he'd sit by the radio, transcribing tunes he'd hear live, and how if he heard a piece in passing only to find out he couldn't get the music, he'd "complain bitterly.") As early as 1934 Messer actively pursued collections of notated violin music as well, on October 20 of that year ordering *Kerr's Collection for Violin* from Ye Olde Firme of Heintzman and Co., Limited, in Toronto. (They, in turn, ordered the books from Scotland.) And by the late 1930s he habitually organized the tunes he liked to play in "scribbler" sized manuscript books, his notation always neat and precise. He always had a penchant for list making, when it came to keeping track of his music. In 1932, in a small notebook from Dominion Life Assurance Co. of Waterloo, Ontario, he wrote out sets of tunes he planned to play, under the word "Programs" (amidst grocery lists including such items as Turnips, Roasters and Butter).

Messer also collected (or was sent) what might be called fiddle-obilia, from Maritime poet Alden A. Nowlan's tribute to his father the fiddler, written in 1960 for the *Atlantic Advocate* ("The fiddles are dancing stars of laughter in a vast black pool of sadness and night," wrote Nowlan), to a treatise on the work of Stradivarius. His collection included texts such as the seventh edition of *The Violin and How To Master It (By a Professional Player)*. This small volume, kept lovingly in one of Messer's scrapbooks, might have reassured him that his stint with classical studies was ample when, on page four, it suggested the following: "The question is often asked by ardent lovers of the violin, Is it possible to learn to play it without a teacher? I have no hesitation in answering that, with steady application, quickness, and observation, it is. But, just as a person may learn to read French by the aid of books alone, but must hear the language spoken before a complete mastery is acquired, so the student of the violin must at least *see* good players performing."

As well as collecting anything related to fiddling, Messer also kept abreast of music news that might have an impact on his own career, with a subscription to *The Composer* (a magazine which declared, in 1945, "It is our duty to see that Canadian music is performed — so that our boys who come home will find that we have done something for them") and to *Roundup: News of Cowboys and Hillbilly Stars of Radio, Records and Screen*, as well as other specialty music publications.

Ultimately, Messer's thorough pursuit of his musical niche, and his orderly, businesslike attitude to life contributed to the kind of musician he was, as well. Duke Nielsen's son Gary would recall that in the *Jubilee* years, when the rest of the band would take a coffee or cigarette break, Messer would often stay behind in the studio, practising one lick over and over again, making sure he had it nailed. It was this precision that contributed to making his style so recognizable.

Messer's strengths as a player are viewed differently, depending on the perspective of the listener. Classical violinist Ed Minevich, who listened to Messer's recordings for the first time at the end of the 20th century, would say: "He was flawless, technically. He had flawless intonation, which is not always the case with fiddlers. He brought fiddling to a much higher level."

Sudbury-based fiddler Don Reed, famed for his work with country stars Dwight Yoakam and Buck Owens, among others, would say that Messer's style was "less ornamented" than some others, that it's as though he "took those fiddle tunes and kind of straightened them out in a way." Another fiddler, Bill Guest, wrote in a paper called *Down East Fiddling*, published by the *Canadian Folk Music Bulletin*, that Messer could "take a traditional tune, make a few changes in it and make it a better tune." Guest's example was the *Firemen's Reel*, the lead-in to the famous *Barndance* theme, which Guest felt that Messer played "smoother" than others.

Folklorists have also taken their turn at defining Messer's style, Dorothy and Homer Hogan suggesting it was a new synthesis of various Canadian traditions, while Edith Fowke went on record suggesting his playing was "simpler" than some others.

George A. Proctor, on the other hand, felt Messer played with "technical polish," evidence of a "sophistication of a basically unsophisticated art," one honed through its communication via a commercialized mass media — recordings, radio and particularly television. There's no question radio and television had a profound affect on Messer's approach to music — to maintain his popularity he felt he had to respond to what his audience praised (which often meant doing things the same way, again and again), and there were other, technical demands as well, such as knowing exactly how many bars of music at any given tempo would equal exactly how many seconds. This knowledge enabled him to be the musical equivalent of some of the CBC's most talented program hosts, who, in broadcasting parlance could "talk to time," making the end of each program segment seem effortless, even when live-to-air. Messer, you could say, knew how to "play to time."

But some believe that not all fiddlers across the country were enamored of Don Messer in his day. According to Ken Perlman, author of *The Fiddle Music of Prince Edward Island* (as quoted in an article by Rick McGinnis in the *Globe and Mail* in 1998), "Older fiddlers, who had come to resent Don Messer for his virtual hegemony over the air waves, which left little room for other fiddlers or styles to be heard, found themselves trying to revive PEI fiddle playing in a younger generation…"

Messer's "hegemony" didn't stop many fiddlers from thrilling to his successes though, or at least wanting to be a part of them. Legendary Métis fiddler Andy DeJarlis (whose music Messer recorded on an LP in 1973, called *A Tribute to Manitoba's Golden Boy Andy DeJarlis*), wrote to Messer in 1971 saying "I do not believe that no other old time fiddler appreciates more your little wee smile as you are doing the work of a master of the early settlers' music."

Plenty of other fiddlers appreciated Messer's work with the early settlers' music too, and his habit of promoting the best of the new, based on the old. They wrote tunes and submitted them to Messer in hopes of airplay, and over the years he gradually built up repertoire based in part upon the contributions of these fiddling fans and colleagues. Messer was, as has been noted, himself a composer, and an occasional co-composer as well, writing a few tunes with none other than Charlie Chamberlain in the early years, including a song called *"Goin'Back"*, with words by L.A. MacDonald. But Messer was not prolific, which may have contributed to his interest in cultivating the work of others. One instance of this was a tune written for Messer by a fiddler named Cohn J. Boyd, called *"Little Burnt Potato"*, which many years later became the subject of an investigation into the process of the aural tradition, through a paper by David Ennis called *Fiddling in Lanark County: A Medium for the Examination of Acculturation in Canadian Folk Music*. Despite what the title of that paper might lead you to believe though, Messer has not been the subject of excessive scrutiny by academics — quite the opposite in fact — but he certainly has been taken very seriously by the few who have made inquiries.

Neil V. Rosenberg, of the folklore department at Memorial University of Newfoundland, has done the most extensive academic work on Messer to date. He observed that a key contribution of Messer's was not so much the style of his playing as the creation of what Rosenberg called a "national fiddle canon," a body of repertoire, popularized by Messer's broadcasts and known to most fiddlers across the country — an extraordinarily significant achievement for any one musician.

While the Violin Slept

Fiddler Earl Mitton, a guest on the *Jubilee* and a colleague of Messer's, paid his old friend a visit in 1971. Afterwards he wrote a letter, commenting, "You have some nice fiddles there and I still like the sound of the one you use on T.V. and I guess it's because I have listened to it for so long that I have gotten used to it."

You could take the comment as almost a slight against the violin, or you could take it as the truest words ever spoken. Classical violinist Ed Minevich would suggest it's the latter, believing that every good violinist makes a kind of marriage with their instrument — and this marriage is not necessarily about the actual quality of the violin. "Don Messer's violin," Minevich said, "Was just right for him, just right for what he did, for that kind of music."

What happened to "that kind of music" though, once Don Messer died? Messer aside, fiddling was losing ground in the 1960s to that other stringed instrument, the guitar, or more specifically, the electric guitar. As fiddler Andy DeJarlis put it, quoted in the *Halifax Mail Star* in 1968, "The voice and guitar of the country and western singer now is on the highway, and the fiddler, right now, is in the ditch." Still, fiddling kept gamely hiking along, finding its most dependable audience via fiddle competitions. These competitions existed as early as the 1920s, but were largely a post-war phenomenon, growing over the years in popularity, with the best known being the Canadian Open Old Time Fiddle Contest in Shelburne, Ontario. (Won by the likes of Messer colleagues Ned Landry, Johnny

Mooring, Al Cherney, Ward Allan, Graham Townsend, and, more recently, younger performers who were influenced by Messer, including Don Reed, Frank Leahy and April Verch.) But after Messer's death, the jigs, reels, breakdowns and hornpipes so celebrated on his television show never again reached the kind of widespread, mainstream audience they did during the heyday of the *Jubilee*.

Then, in the waning years of the 20th century, two things happened that proved fiddle music could still be part of mainstream North American culture. Both exploded at around the same time, circa 1995: Riverdance and Ashley MacIsaac. Riverdance, the spawn of the highly influential Eurovision Song Contest, and a triumph of marketing, popularized Irish dance, and as a byproduct, drew attention to Celtic music of all kinds. It enabled anyone who played a jig or a reel or did any form of step dancing to have sudden new cachet. As for Ashley MacIsaac, the prodigiously talented fiddler from Creignish, Cape Breton, he blew apart any notions of quaint traditions of bygone days. Dressed in army boots and combat pants (or kilts), and fusing the fiddle tunes of his youth with the "grunge" of the day, MacIsaac toured widely as a kind of rock star, accompanied by rock-staresque shenanigans.

But while MacIsaac was indisputably the most famous, or perhaps infamous, of fiddling rockers, he certainly was not alone in his interest in fusing the old with the new. The late, Newfoundland-born fiddler Martyn Bennett, who moved to Scotland when he was a boy, was mixing up electronica with traditional tunes to great success in Europe at about the same time as MacIsaac stormed North America. All of it, Riverdance and the fiddling young rockers, hugely accelerated an already existing Celtic revival, with headlines such as *Billboard Magazine*'s, *"Cashing In On Celtic,"* or CNN's on-line equivalent, *"World's Playing Along With Frenzied Fiddlers of Celtic Music."* What it ultimately meant was that fiddling continued to have a small but tenacious toe-hold in the world of pop music, as it moved into the 21st century.

Other, gentler forms of fusion have also prevailed, many from prominent Canadian fiddlers, including Frank Leahy's blends of classical and folk traditions; Natalie MacMaster's treatments of Cape Breton fiddling alongside styles such as bluegrass; or the music of Ottawa Valley fiddler April Verch, who has found inspiration in a multiplicity of fiddle styles, as well as in music from a range of traditions. Verch, who was born five years after Don Messer died, has observed that since that time, fiddle playing has evolved in such a way as to blur some of the former stylistic distinctions.

"It used to be that people would play a style, Cape Breton or French Canadian or old-time Canadian," Verch has said, "But now it's more difficult to call anyone anything that specific." Verch would chalk this up to increased travel, and a plethora of fiddle camps where people come from around the world to play and exchange tunes. Like all players of her generation, she grew up in an era when many fiddlers wrote new compositions, and found it "cool" to play these newer pieces. But in her case, older fiddlers, hearing her play at competitions, would remind her that it was important to understand where the tradition came from. "Listen to Don Messer," they'd tell her. She did. And what's more, she continues to tell her young fiddle students the same thing.

I Let My Fiddle Do The Talking

Although Don Messer is no longer the Canadian household name he once was, from coast to coast to coast, his legacy lives on in every descendent of every Messer fan, and, if performers such as Verch, Leahy or Reed get their way, every subsequent generation of fiddlers. Don Reed would take it further, saying: "Everybody that's playing Canadian fiddle has part of that Don Messer thinking in their playing, whether they realize it or not. It's just so much a part of Canadian fiddling there's no way you can escape that influence."

Many have wanted not only to *not* escape it, but also to celebrate that influence. In fact the power of Messer's story and of the music of the

Islanders has inspired subsequent generations of artists to create stories based on this part of Canadian music history.

Playwright John Gray, for example, composed an original musical called *Don Messer's Jubilee*, which had several successful runs in Canadian theatres in the mid-and late 1980s. Frank Leahy also created a stage play called *Don Messer's Violin*, in 2000, a re-enactment of a rehearsal and performance of *Don Messer's Jubilee*, as well as an encapsulated version of how the famous program met its end. Leahy had the daunting task of both (literally) playing Don Messer's violin, and acting the role of Messer, but he took it so well in stride that the government of Prince Edward Island declared it a "mega hit" after the show's first season. The legacy of Don Messer and His Islanders, it would seem, is one that continues to inspire and provoke strong feelings, and the interest of audiences in the music has clearly not died.

Perhaps the most successful tribute of all to date has been a recording made by CBC Records in 2000, by Frank Leahy, also called *Don Messer's Violin*. It features music made famous by Messer as well as some Leahy originals, all played on Don Messer's violin. The recording became one of the best-selling CBC releases in the label's history. Messer's long-running television producer, Bill Langstroth, penned the liner notes for Leahy's recording, and offered this assessment of the work that the musicians and producers created. "I sense, too, their collective delight in being connected to Mr. Messer's legacy," Langstroth wrote, "The circle *is* unbroken."

Epilogue

For all the words spoken and written about the popularity of *Don Messer's Jubilee*, relatively little has been published about the man himself. It's not surprising, given that Messer tended to be a man of so few words. Well chosen words, mind you, and sometimes etched with a humour so dry that interviewers invariably missed the quiet asides as they slipped on by. Nonetheless, Messer made for a challenging interview, and continues, posthumously, to be something of an enigma.

No doubt Messer had a number of reasons why he disliked being in the spotlight (when he wasn't performing), and why he rarely chose to speak to the camera or into a microphone. The assumption has typically been that he was too shy, or that his reserve stemmed from being such a deeply private person. Certainly the latter seems an accurate assessment of his personality. But his reticence was also born out of something else, out of deciding first and foremost to honour his calling — in other words, the music. A writer named Frank Sullivan with the *Winnipeg Tribune* did an astute job of summing this up, back in 1965:

"Not much has been said about Don Messer. That's the way he prefers it. While pushing his group to the forefront, either in solos or in combinations, he remains in the background where, he says, 'I let my fiddle do the talking for me.' "

For Canadians, fans who loved the music of Don Messer, it was all he ever really needed to say.

Sources

Archives, Libraries, Foundations

Canadian Broadcasting Corporation Reference Library, Toronto, Ontario
Canadian Communications Foundation in Association with Ryerson University, Toronto, Ontario
Library and Archives Canada, Ottawa, Ontario
Nova Scotia Archives and Records Management, Halifax, Nova Scotia
University of New Brunswick Libraries, Fredericton, New Brunswick

Film, Video, Audio

CFCY Radio Shows, circa 1940s (CFCY Radio)
Don Messer: His Land and His Music (National Film Board of Canada), 1971
Don Messer's Jubilee (Visual Resources, CBC)
The Good Old Days, Apex TVLP 79052-1979
The Jubilee Years (Visual Resources, CBC)
Life and Times, Don Messer (CBC Television), 2001

Print and Online

American Music: A Panorama, by Daniel Kingman, New York: Schirmer Books, 1979
Canada, a National History, by Margaret Conrad and Alvin Finkel, Toronto: Pearson Education Canada, 2003
Canada's Don Messer by Lester B. Sellick, Kentville, N.S. Publishing, 1969
"Conflicting Visions: Don Messer, Liberal Nationalism and the Canadian Unity Debate", by Joahnne Devlin Trew, *International Journal of Canadian Studies*, 2002
Country Music, The Rough Guide, by Kurt Wolff, London: Rough Guides Ltd., 2000
Crossings, the Great Transatlantic Migrations, 1870-1914, by Walter Nugent, Bloomington, Indiana: Indiana University Press, 1992
"Don Messer's Modern Canadian Fiddle Canon", by Neil V. Rosenberg, *Canadian Folk Music Journal*, 1994
"Down East Fiddling", by Bill Guest, *Canadian Folk Music Bulletin*, 1985
The Encyclopedia of Music in Canada, Toronto: University of Toronto Press, 1992
"The Fall and Rise of the Cape Breton Fiddler: 1955-1982", by Marie Thompson, unpublished M.A. thesis, 2003
"Fiddling in Lanark County: A Medium for the Examination of Acculturation in Canadian Folk Music", by David Ennis, *Canadian Journal for Traditional Music*, 1987

"Fiddling in Western Manitoba: A Preliminary Report", by Anne Lederman, *Canadian Folk Music Bulletin*, 1985

History of the Canadian Peoples, Volume II, by Alvin Finkel and Margaret Conrad, Toronto: Copp Clark Ltd., 1998

The Illustrated History of Canada, Edited By Craig Brown, Toronto: Lester & Orpen Dennys Limited, 1987

"Lumbercamp Singing and the Two Traditions", by Edward D. Ives, *Canadian Journal for Traditional Music*, 1977

The Microphone Wars, a History of Triumph and Betrayal at the CBC, by Knowlton Nash, Toronto: McClelland & Stewart, 1994

"Old-Time Fiddling in New Brunswick", by Ivan C. Hicks, *Canadian Folk Music Bulletin*, 1985

Old-Time Fiddling in Ontario, by George A. Proctor, National Museums of Canada, 1963

Out of Thin Air: The Story of CFCY "The Friendly Voice of the Maritimes," by Betty Rogers Large and Tom Crothers, Charlottetown, P.E.I.: Applecross Press, 1989

The Peoples Of Canada, A Post-Confederation History, by J.M. Bumsted, Toronto: Oxford University Press, 1992

"Repetition, Innovation, and Representation in Don Messer's Media Repertoire", by Neil V. Rosenberg, *Journal of American Folklore*, 2002

Remembering Singalong Jubilee, by Ernest J. Dick, Formac Publishing Company, 2004

"A Survey of Fiddling on Prince Edward Island", by Jim Hornby, *Canadian Folk Music Bulletin*, 1985

Violin-making, as it Was, and Is, by Ed Heron-Allen, Ward Lock Limited, reprinted in 1976

"WBZ's Early History" by Donna L. Halper, <www.bostonradio.org> 2002

When Television Was Young, Primetime Canada 1952-1967, by Paul Rutherford, Toronto: University of Toronto Press, 1990

Index